Take Two

A story of
baby adoptions

Take Two

A story of baby adoptions

LAUREL ASHTON

Published by
British Association for Adoption & Fostering
(BAAF)
Saffron House
6–10 Kirby Street
London EC1N 8TS
www.baaf.org.uk

Charity registration 275689 (England & Wales) and
SC039337 (Scotland)

British Library Cataloguing in Publication Data
A catalogue record for this book is available from the
British Library

ISBN 978 1 9(

Project manage
Cover design b
Designed by A
Typeset by Fra
Printed in Gre
Trade distribut
Olympia Tradi

WORCESTERSHIRE
COUNTY COUNCIL

220

Bertrams   01/06/2009

362.734   £7.95

EV

The moral right of the author has been asserted in accordance with
the Copyright, Designs and Patents Act 1988.

BAAF is the leading UK-wide membership organisation for all
those concerned with adoption, fostering and child care issues.

The paper used for the text pages of this book is FSC certified.
FSC (The Forest Stewardship Council) is an international network
to promote responsible management of the world's forests.

Printed on totally chlorine-free paper.

FSC
Mixed Sources
Product group from well-managed
forests and other controlled sources

Cert no. SGS-COC-2482
www.fsc.org
© 1996 Forest Stewardship Council

Acknowledgements

I am grateful to Hedi Argent for helping me complete this book and to BAAF for publishing it. I am especially indebted to Carole Waters, not only for taking the time to read the manuscript, but also for all her advice and enthusiasm over the past few years. In addition, I would like to thank all the women (and occasional brave man) on the Adoption and Fostering Forum of *Babyworld.co.uk*, who have been an invaluable source of support throughout this whole process. Thanks also go to all of our friends and family for just being there when we needed them, and especially to Marion, who took me on lovely long walks and let me ramble on for hours. My parents, now Grandma and Grandpa, deserve a special mention for their encouragement and loving help, and not least for painting the entire house just days before Amber arrived.

Some names and details of events have been changed for the purpose of publication in order to protect identity.

About the author

Laurel Ashton was born in Lincolnshire in 1968. She is married to David and lives in the Midlands with their two children. She works in higher education.

The Our Story series

This book is part of BAAF's Our Story series, which explores adoption experiences as told by adoptive parents.

Also available in this series:

- *An Adoption Diary: A couple's journey from infertility to parenthood* by Maria James
- *Flying Solo: A single parent's adoption story* by Julia Wise
- *In Black and White: The story of an open transracial adoption* by Nathalie Seymour
- *Adoption Undone: A painful story of an adoption breakdown* by Karen Carr
- *Together in Time: How creative therapies helped a family who adopted two boys with attachment difficulties* by Ruth and Ed Royce
- *The Family Business: The story of a family's adoption of a boy with cerebral palsy* by Robert Marsden.

The series editor

Hedi Argent is an independent family placement consultant, trainer and freelance writer. She is the author of *Find me a Family* (Souvenir Press, 1984), *Whatever Happened to Adam?* (BAAF, 1998), *Related by Adoption* (BAAF, 2004), *Ten Top Tips for Placing Children in Families* (BAAF, 2006), *Ten Top Tips for Placing Siblings* (2008), and *Josh and Jaz have Three Mums* (2007), the co-author of *Taking Extra Care* (BAAF, 1997, with Ailee Kerrane), and *Dealing with Disruption* (BAAF, 2006, with Jeffrey Coleman), and the editor of *Keeping the Doors Open* (BAAF, 1988), *See You Soon* (BAAF, 1995), *Staying Connected* (BAAF, 2002), and *Models of Adoption Support* (BAAF, 2003). She has also written five illustrated booklets in the children's series published by BAAF: *What Happens in Court?* (2003, with Mary Lane), *What is Contact?* (2004), *What is a Disability?* (2004), *Life Story Work* (2005, with Shaila Shah) and *Kinship Care* (2007).

This book is of course dedicated with all my love to my wonderful husband and fabulous children.

Sometimes you have to catch what life throws at you...

Contents

Foreword

This is the account of one couple's compelling journey towards parenthood and beyond. It encompasses not only the joy of becoming an adoptive parent, but also the trials and tribulations of just *being* a parent!

Most women have an innate need to reproduce, and to nurture their own baby. Of course, some women may choose not to have children, but when that choice is taken away, it is one of the worst things that can happen to a woman. You suddenly feel that you are an outsider in a world that you so desperately want to join. You are unable to achieve the most natural thing in the world – giving birth to a baby. And it hurts, unbelievably so! But you do have another choice: you can either set out to heal yourself and live a childless life or you can take another route to becoming a parent – adoption!

Baby adoptions were far more common 50 years ago when infants were often relinquished to avoid the stigma of being a young unmarried mother and bringing "shame" on the family. Of course, in the 21st century, these concerns have been replaced by new ones: not many babies are voluntarily relinquished – they are more likely to be taken into the care of local authorities when parents are deemed to be incapable of looking after their children. With a court order in place, social workers are then able to look for suitable parents for each child.

Another difference from long ago is that secrecy no longer surrounds adoption. In recent years, social services have changed their policies to encourage, where possible, continuing contact with the birth parents and extended birth family. It is felt that it will help the children to feel more secure and stable if they do not have to deal with unanswered questions and a big gap where their family history would be. Adopted children are now given a life story book, which helps them to understand their background and birth family history. As adoptive parents, we have a responsibility to assist our children in coming to terms with what might be a difficult story to read.

Most childless couples who decide to adopt hope to adopt a baby. This is understandable, but can be another stumbling block on an already tiring and what feels like a relentless journey. At the beginning of the process you are told, in no uncertain terms, that very few babies are available. Most children spend at least a year in care before the lengthy process to release them for adoption is complete. Therefore most children are usually well over a year old before they are placed, and much older if they have spent a significant amount of time in the birth family home.

However, baby adoptions do still happen, and contrary to popular belief, an adopter's age is not necessarily a deciding factor.

The adoption process is fraught with frustration and interwoven with joy. It is another emotional roller-coaster to endure in your quest to become parents – but at the end of this one, you will probably achieve your goal. However, there are no guarantees, and things can and do go wrong. Working well with your social worker is paramount: it is important to understand why assessments have to be intrusive and explorative, and to realise that you are truly working towards the best interests of the child. Your child-to-be. It can be quite a shock to realise that this isn't all about you.

Laurel's book is an open, honest, beautifully written account focusing on adoption, but also dealing with the pain of infertility. Many such stories, fact or fiction, end in a surprise pregnancy, but this book shows that there are other happy endings. Being an adopter myself, I found that a refreshing change, and I also found myself smiling, laughing and crying along with Laurel. At times, I almost felt I was reading my own story.

This book will not only move the reader, but will also give an insight into adoption and all that it entails. It will help those who are still in the process of completing their own journey towards parenthood, and for those who have come out the other side, it will offer a nostalgic read.

Carole Waters
Adoptive parent to Bea, now aged two-and-a-half
Moderator of the Babyworld Adoption and Fostering Forum
(www.babyworld.co.uk)
October 2008

1

The baby bug bites

Our decision to put off the baby stage was never a conscious one. Other things just happened. We spent too long being educated, did too much living and travelling and indulged our love of being together. No one ever told us that we might regret this foot-dragging, lackadaisical approach to parenthood. We just knew that we would be ready one day. Some day. In the meantime, life was kind. We were moderately successful professionals, typical thirty-somethings enjoying our friends, dinners and numerous hobbies. We lived in a very adult world. Come to think of it, we had no children around us. Teaching Italian at college to eighteen-year-olds was the closest I came to children. David had given up his job as a teacher to become a full-time writer and was finally beginning to see some moderate success. Shockingly, a few friends had suddenly become parents, but we remained among a group of people who were free to roam from one dinner to another, meet in the bar at the cinema and gather at an eclectic selection of classical, jazz and rock concerts. Not that we disliked children. On the rare occasions when they entered our life, we would run, dance, clown and eat cake and sweets. We never changed nappies. We never accepted overnight responsibility for unaccompanied minors. And we never had to worry.

Then the baby bug simply hit us. No discussion. No concerns. Just the most natural, organic, lovely decision that two people can make. Overnight we were ready to take on the biggest commitment of our lives. We were both satisfied with work; liked our little house; were financially solvent; visited the gym two to three times a week; and even grew our own organic vegetables on our modest allotment. Now all we needed was a baby. We skipped the gym and sports to engage in our new pastime of babymaking. After all, it would only be for a couple of months. Or so we thought. Those first few weeks were very exciting. We would rush home from work early, call off drinks with friends, leave the car unwashed and house un-vacuumed, to make love at every possible moment. At the end of the first two weeks of trying, I sat on the side of the bath waiting for the pregnancy test to show up positive. Could be. Couldn't be. Could be. Couldn't be. It was the longest couple of minutes. I went downstairs to tell David the bad news.

'Never mind,' he said. We were just warming up.

Even the second failure didn't bother us. We were enjoying ourselves and, although disappointed, we were not really concerned when yet again the test turned out to be negative. By the third month of trying, though, we were both secretly beginning to wonder if there was something physically wrong with one or both of us. But then I developed every symptom I could imagine: sore breasts, headaches, slight nausea. I had started seeing a reflexologist, Shaheen, and she boosted my hopes still further that month when she felt a puffiness under the balls of my feet and said that it could be a sign. My head, thyroid and hormone areas were all very sensitive too, she said. Sure indications. Frustratingly, although we are frequently reminded that science has come a long way, it is still impossible to tell for sure whether or not a woman is pregnant before her period is due. Even when I started to feel the low grumbling of my week-before-period pains, it was impossible not to believe that I was pregnant. I succumbed, inevitably, to doing a ridiculously early pregnancy test. I willed the second line to appear. Of course it did not. But then I convinced myself that I must have tested too early. I did three more tests, squandering more money. David, slightly disappointed that I had not invited him to the first non-showing, attended the rest. No. No. And no. If I had been honest with myself, even before my period my imaginary signs had all gone. Except for my feet, which I now realise are naturally puffy and fat. My breasts were sore from being prodded and pulled all the time and the headaches and nausea must have come from sheer tension. When the bleeding finally started, I headed straight for the gym to do the hardest aerobic workout and punish my body for torturing my mind. My self-imposed busy spell continued with a mad spate of tiling and painting, swallowing dust fumes and coating my face and hair in clouds of lilac emulsion. This frenetic activity did not actually make me feel any better, but the new bathroom looked great. It was going to be exhausting to spend every month in such a state of anticipation.

At the start of month number four, we decided to take drastic action. We would give up caffeine, alcohol and chocolate. Our plan did last for a few days and we did cut down, although a few treats slipped through our fingers. I started to read snippets in magazines, newspapers and online about how to conceive effectively. Every article and radio programme screamed at us to "Relax". But it is hard to take it easy when you are being forced to be calm. And so we then began to worry about not being sufficiently relaxed. One of the bitter ironies of the whole of that time for me was the continued pain I had to suffer every month. Some women call their period "Aunt Flo"; for me it's definitely a man. My "old man". He is tall and stooped, walks with a heavy stick and knocks loudly at my door exactly one week before he makes his angry appearance. I have always had problems with him. At school he routinely got me out of class, and I would be escorted, pale, sometimes green, by a posse of friends to matron's office. As I grew older the pain became less frequent and my relationship with the old man mellowed. The pill was never an option for me: partly because it was offered to me at the age of fifteen when I believed it was something only adult and sexually active women should even contemplate; and partly because I have been a crusader for natural remedies for most of my life. In any case, I acknowledged subconsciously that it was thanks to my old man that I would one day be able to have a baby. And, according to my mother's many knowledgeable friends, after my first child the pains would go away.

No one prepares you for trying to have children. Surrounded by images of all sorts of families from the perfect to the dysfunctional, we are never really taught the ins and outs of the babymaking process. For many couples it just happens, and often by accident. For others, it does take a while, a few months of practice. But for a significant minority, there is a whole lot more waiting in store. After four months of pretending to be nonchalant about the process, we decided to replace our guestimating of dates with the accuracy of science. To be on the safe side, I bought an ovulation predictor kit, a further investment in our project. Spontaneous passion was soon to become a thing of the past and before long our life was directed by thin blue lines. I duly looked for my "surge," indicating the best time to have sex, just before I ovulated. Of course I started using the predictor sticks too soon and only had one left to try when there was still no sign of impending ovulation. When the last ovulator stick told me that the surge had come, we suddenly felt under pressure to maximise our chances. We did everything we could. After sex I would even spend half an hour with my legs up and pillows under my backside. By this point, we started to wonder if we were getting carried away a bit. But, at certain times in life, all old wives' tales are truths to be believed and respected.

Six months had soon passed. We said nothing to each other, preferring to hide our nagging suspicions. I tried to tell myself that I was just being impatient. Perhaps we had not timed our activities accurately. Or perhaps we had been too tired, or in the wrong positions. We told no one. I sneaked a look at a few magazines and I knew that average couples take up to a year to conceive. So far, then, we were still "normal." The problem was that we knew we were following our dates fairly accurately, making love at every possible moment, taking folic acid and zinc. But our biggest problem was that we just hadn't expected it to be this difficult. Babies are everywhere you look. Our mediocrity was brought home to us acutely as we became swamped by other people's success stories. Alex and Jackie were suddenly and unexpectedly having twins; even Colin and Dasha, who had been trying for ages, finally got the blue line. She told us, now smug but oblivious to our circumstances, that it happens for couples who want it badly enough. That became one of my least favourite comments.

The expensive ovulation kits did not seem to be helping either. I tried to listen to my body and knew that I was not pregnant. One evening, when David was at a meeting, I felt myself deflating. Why couldn't we have a child? I was supposed to be writing up class notes, but started surfing the web for infertility sites. I found far too many. Babyworld.co.uk, which I would cling to for the months – and years – to follow, included the whole baby experience and I joined the "trying for a baby" discussion board. At first I just lurked, reading message after message from women (and occasionally men) who were as frustrated as I was. Almost all of them had been trying for a baby for several months and I logged off feeling quite the novice, convinced that I would never get to their stages. I read a newspaper article about the number of women and couples who have decided that they don't want babies. They were complaining that they feel socially marginalised, as work and home create expectations and laws around child care and family life. Even politicians tell us that this is how we should be living. The article listed reasons why people choose not to have children, with the caveat that 'in a minority of cases it's because of infertility'. People who desperately want children but can't have them feel even more excluded. Many of them pretend that they are in the "not wanting kids right now" group, so as to avoid all the intrusive questions. But at the same time, they are surrounded by colleagues and friends complaining that work or home life doesn't give them enough rights or time to do this or that with their children. Infertile couples live in a social grey zone in which they have no voice and sneak around in embarrassed silence. Had we really joined that group? No way, I told myself.

By the seventh month I was beginning to go through alternating waves of happiness and worry. I would be walking down the street, cooking dinner or at work and find myself drifting off with thoughts of introducing our baby to the world. I nurtured a recurrent daydream, in which a beautiful blonde-haired little girl in a blue dress runs ahead of me towards the duck pond. I run after her, laughing, catch her up in my arms and swing her round, and at that precise moment bump into an old school friend. I introduce her to my daughter. That's it. I just want to tell someone, 'This is my child'.

Another couple of months passed as we kept trying, with and without thermometers, kits, pillows and herbal remedies. I didn't want David to see me upset; it was bad enough that I was working myself up into a state and there seemed little point in worrying him with my anxieties. What I didn't think about was how *he* might be feeling. I would wait until he went out, make sure I got home before him, or stay up later on the pretext of work, and sit in an almost overflowing bubble bath to do my crying. In candlelight and a haze of aromatherapy oils, I released all my sadness through quiet sobs and uncontrollable shivers. After about half an hour I would get out, dry myself briskly, soak my toad-like eyes in cold water, douse myself with body lotion and get on with my life. But that deep sadness was never far away and I could feel it growing month by month. I still kept telling myself that I was being impatient and ridiculous, but the pressure inside would not subside. Then one night David came home earlier than expected and surprised me as I lay in the dark on the sofa in the lounge. He said nothing, just took off his coat, sat down beside me and opened his arms.

'I know,' was all that he kept repeating.

That night when we eventually went to bed, we fell asleep tightly wrapped together. The following morning he brought me a glass of orange juice and a bowl of muesli in bed, something he had never once done in our seven-and-a-half years of marriage. He must be worried about me, I thought, but I said,

'Shall we talk about it?'

'I think we've bottled this up for long enough, don't you?'

I told him how hard I was finding it to get through a single day without thinking about children or being reminded that we don't have any. And he told me that he felt exactly the same. Somehow, he said, he was failing me. Wasn't he supposed to be husband and father? He was surrounded by men with children and was surprised at how he felt. He'd never cared what anyone thought of him, until now. He was starting to feel really worthless and that he was letting me down. How could he be a man if he couldn't be a father? 'I just don't know what to do.'

We were both numb for about ten minutes. And then we talked. And talked. For about five hours. David told me about a couple of friends from his publishers who had gone on holiday and got pregnant "by accident", about how annoyed he was that they viewed it as an inconvenience.

And that for him, just as for me, hearing other people tell their innocent baby stories could sometimes make him feel deeply sad and deeply inadequate. We were exhausted but liberated, finally realising that not only could we be totally honest with one another, but that we had to be open if we wanted things to get better. Whatever that might mean. We reviewed our predicament and set out our options. It was, we agreed, too soon to go to the doctors. What we needed was a holiday. And so the following morning after a couple of hours on the internet, we booked a flight to Rome for the half-term break, hired a car and reserved a room for a couple of nights along the coast. We would improvise the rest. After all our recent planning, we did not want to be too organised.

We had a beautiful holiday and it was wonderful to worry only about what to visit each day, where to eat and who would do the driving. We negotiated the rocky coastline, drove inland and up hills and found hidden treasures of family restaurants. Only by being away did we realise how stressed we had made ourselves, fitting in emergency love-making sessions around work and ironing. Taking a break gave us the chance not only to evaluate what it all meant and how we could deal with it, but also to enjoy just being with each other. Yet those baby thoughts were never far away and in the romantic moonlit setting of our room, with its white muslin drapes swaying against the open window, I started involuntarily to work out my cycle dates and knew that we should be more or less in the zone. Perfect. We could call the baby Amalfi. And what an idyllic conception. We congratulated ourselves on our best ever holiday and were sure that we felt revitalised and hassle-free and ready for that pursuit of parenthood. Which may even be round the corner, I secretly convinced myself. My biggest dream, one that had been fermenting as we walked hand in hand from one beautiful seafront to the next, was that I would be ready to tell my mother of her impending grandmother status. That news would make the perfect present for her sixtieth birthday in three weeks' time.

The holiday had not, after all, worked magic. If anything, it convinced us that we really did have a problem. If we couldn't conceive in such an idyllic place with no other distractions and any anxieties washed away by moonlight, how would we manage being back at home and work? Some things in life are meant to be difficult: going for promotion or a new job; looking for a partner; buying a house. But everyone has babies, you only have to read the statistics on unwanted pregnancies to know that it is only too easy to conceive. It's not supposed to be impossible. When you fail month after month to become pregnant, the most difficult thing is to sustain optimism, to pretend that you are not consumed by it all. We jumped back into our nightly babymaking. It was hard to find "special occasions"; we just had a special mission. We were running out of ideas for passion at the end of long and hassle-filled working days. And sometimes other things got in the way. One evening when we'd just got into bed, I leant back, screamed, jerked up and hit David's chin with the crown of my head. He was left nursing his face as I hopped round the room naked, trying to understand what had happened. My back swelled up instantly and any other thoughts dissolved. Somehow a wasp had got into the bed. This babymaking project was turning into a series of comedy sketches.

After all those efforts, I decided that I was growing far too introspective about the whole thing and, more importantly, needed to stop looking accusingly at all those unhealthy looking people with babies. I would find myself glaring at screaming mothers in supermarkets and staring incredulously at miserable looking families in the street. It was certainly time to consider the next stage.

I met David for lunch in our favourite park, where we sat on a bench under the cradling branches of an oak tree, out of the cool breeze. I had packed a thermos of tea and some cheese sandwiches. We both knew what we planned to talk about, but put it off with tales about his publisher and my star student. Suddenly I changed the subject.

'I think we should make a doctor's appointment.'

'But they won't see us until we've been trying for over a year.'

'Are you sure?'

'Yes. We have to give it a bit longer.'

'But we both know something is wrong, and we're not getting any younger at thirty three.'

'I know. I suppose we could lie, say that we've been trying for a lot longer.'

'OK. I agree, but let's give it a couple more months before we decide to go down that route.'

We also decided to cool our panic: the ban on alcohol and caffeine was lifted entirely and there was to be no mention of predictor kits or ovulation. We both wanted to let nature take over. And we agreed to associate not getting pregnant with positive little outcomes, such as presents or weekends away.

Meanwhile, it was my mother's sixtieth birthday party, which I had been planning for about six months. Fifty of her friends gathered in a local hotel, complete with a rock and roll band to play her favourite oldies. As she danced the night away, laughing and happy, I felt miserable inside. The one present I wanted to give her was the one thing I could not. Perhaps she would rather have the weekend in Venice my brother and I had bought her anyway. But I suspected that one grandchild would be worth a million trips to Italy. The following day she and I went for a walk around her Yorkshire village and gossiped about the night before.

'Do you think Liz could have imposed those photos of her grandchildren on any more of the guests?'

She smiled as she spoke, but caught the twinge on my face. She said nothing for a moment and then it finally came out, the question she had been wanting to ask for a very long time:

'Do you think that you and David will ever, well, think about starting a family? I know it's not for everyone, but...' She trailed off.

'We have been trying, for over six months, but with no luck so far.'

I tried to keep my voice as cheerful as possible. We were approaching the village green and passed a gaggle of miserable looking teenagers, draped over a couple of benches and a moped.

'Do you want all that?' my mother nodded, laughing quietly at the broody bunch.

'Desperately,' came the silent response from deep inside me.

I hesitated and for a moment hot tears welled up and I thought I would not be able to stop them. But I held fast, took a deep breath and turned directly to my mum.

'Well, it would be nice.'

We did not talk for the remainder of the walk. Sharing my secret with my mum had removed a huge pressure from my mind, but I knew that it had also forced a new burden on her. I knew she would look at me differently from now on, but at the same time I was greatly relieved to have an ally.

In month nine an unexpected craving for cheese sandwiches got me all worked up with excitement. As usual, all tests were negative and I was probably just salt deficient. Things didn't change in the weeks and months that followed. My old man hates flying and always changes my cycle when I have been travelling. He made me pay for a trip to Milan with an unprecedented thirty-four day cycle. I did about six pregnancy tests, all negative, and got to the point of willing the old misery to return. I went running. Nothing, except a slight nausea and tenderness in my breasts and constant hunger. But still more negatives. I thought I might be going ever so slightly mad. Poor David was forced to listen to me analyse every twinge and sign. He started going to extra pottery classes; I'm sure anything was better than an evening at home with me. I started to feel a horrible lump in my tummy and wondered if it could be my period, or a baby. Or maybe cancer. I scrutinised every tiny internal blip in detail. But nothing had changed, and my old man appeared in his own good time.

Christmas came with that added trial of the family get-together and that was when I learnt that you cannot and must not move from one marker to the next: maybe by my birthday, for my mum's birthday, in our new house, at Christmas, and so on. You only set yourself up for disappointment. I had tried not to fall into the trap, but inevitably, after the failure on Mum's birthday, I drove myself forward with the hope of a Christmas announcement. I had also decided not to say anything straightaway; I would wait until dessert. There would be more than a twenty pence piece in my Christmas pudding. What is more, my period was not due until Christmas Eve, so when I returned from Christmas shopping I desperately wished my exhaustion to be the result of pregnancy and not from the effort of having to force my way through the festive crowds of over-burdened shoppers. What was worse, I noticed that even Christmas shopping is horrid when you see baby clothes and toys everywhere. When my old man inevitably appeared on time, I somehow managed to survive Christmas Day, keeping to myself thoughts about the baby I should have been about to announce. My problem is my romantic imagination, harbouring little vignettes of playing with my baby beneath the Christmas tree. As a friend and mother of a two-year-old later pointed out to me, though, I would be more likely to be catching the falling tree and calming his tantrums.

I was quite tearful for a few days between Christmas and the New Year – another marker – but forced myself to return to a healthy cynicism. Over coffee and croissants on New Year's Day, we had our third serious chat about our problem. We were by now both sure that there was, indeed, a problem. It was time to seek a professional opinion. But again, we put it off until spring, after the busy term I had ahead and David's biggest and most important deadline so far. And yet, at the same time, a weight was lifted from our shoulders. I decided, ignoring my own advice about avoiding markers, to give myself a year to get pregnant, and saw the new year as a new chance. One way or another, I was determined that next Christmas it would be my turn to have "news".

In January, all the imaginary signs returned. But I was not pregnant. David called this one "sag aloo", blaming the whirring noises in my abdomen on the recent spate of curries we had enjoyed. In February an over-energetic front crawl left me with enough "symptoms" of pregnancy to get excited. I prayed to God that he would send me a baby on what would have been my grandmother's birthday. He sent me a bad case of PMT and spots instead. By March, I was not so optimistic about the year. I was getting fed up again, but decided to adopt a new attitude. 'I AM pregnant,' I would tell myself, 'at least until I find out otherwise.'

Nearly a whole year of trying had passed. We didn't celebrate our eighth wedding anniversary as I'd planned it in my mind. Another unavoidable marker. The original idea was to invite the whole family over so that we could announce our good news. I'd decided that I would tell them over homemade rich chocolate mousse. How confident. And how wrong. I went through the motions of setting a beautiful and elaborate table, planning menus, shopping, then cooking for hours and carrying my old man with me all the time. I caved in to painkillers and could have eaten the whole packet that morning as our eight guests arrived: my parents, David's parents, our brothers and their partners. It was a pleasant family scene and I wanted them all to go away. A mean twist of fate turned a bad morning into a terrible afternoon. Over the cheese fondue, David's brother and sister-in-law made their announcement: at the ripe old age of twenty-three she was pregnant and the baby was due in seven months. If they'd

13

smacked me over the head with a large cricket bat it couldn't have hurt more. Andrew is David's younger brother and they'd been competitive with one another since early childhood, over toys, football and records. And for most of that time Andrew had been playing catch-up with a successful elder brother. So when he and Jane got married, they started trying for children straightaway. And now he'd won. How I managed to say Fantastic! Congratulations!, and spray a few kisses in the air, I don't know. I went to fetch the promised bread from the kitchen, where I nearly sliced open my index finger as I tried to cut and cry simultaneously. When I returned, having dried my eyes and resolved to fall apart only later, David's hand gripped mine tightly under the table and I managed a broad smile and more effusive congratulations. Apart from my mother, I fooled them all into thinking I was the happy hostess, even joking lightly in response to Jane's question about when we would start thinking about having children.

'When we can fit them in.'

Ha ha. I kept a firm hold on my glass of red wine and sneaked away with a headache when I could stand it no longer, leaving Jane and Andrew as the *ad hoc* guests of honour. My mother came up to see me, but I pretended to be asleep. I couldn't bear the pity, however well intentioned.

The effects of our anniversary party turned me into a complete idiot. I had started drinking more than usual, just a couple of glasses of wine each evening, but still more than I should. In the "surge" week I drank far too much one night and spent an hour with my head in the toilet bowl. Making love was not an option when even standing up was too painful. I then spent the following day chastising myself and wondering if I could be entirely serious about all this baby business. Thankfully, I was going off to Italy for work for three weeks without David. No husband meant no babymaking pressure. But then I just missed him instead, especially since he was the only one I could talk to about everything. Apart from my parents and David's mum and dad, we had told very few friends about our "problem". My old man arrived while I was away and David sounded very dejected when I spoke to him on the phone and related our monthly bad news. I did chat briefly and fairly casually to my friend in Milan, as she played with her eleven-month-old daughter. Giovanna said I should get a medical check-up. She was probably right, but part of me still didn't want to know for sure what I thought I knew already.

Trying for a baby changes your perception of time. After more than a year of trying to conceive, time had come to be counted in twenty-seven-day units. In the first few months, we would design babies according to when it would be convenient to give birth. We had even initially contemplated skipping a few months of trying, as a baby born in the following summer would waste my chance of maximising maternity leave. I have often wondered if my inability to have children is a punishment for such presumptive calculation.

I was in a hazy state of denial. 'If not this month, then next,' I would hear in my head, my morning mantra. And then I crashed the car while daydreaming. My first thoughts went to my unborn baby. My unconceived baby. I was in denial about everything: denial that I had a problem, and denial that I was worried about having a problem. We decided that we really did need help of a more professional kind. Maybe it was time to graduate from trying for a baby to considering infertility.

2

What else is there?

My sister-in-law sounded cheerfully pregnant on the phone.

'How are you feeling?'

'Great. Getting excited now. And a bit terrified. Well, a lot terrified really. I just want to get it over and done with now, even though there's a way to go.' There was an awkward silence until she continued.

'How are you and David?'

'Really busy at work. Did Andrew tell you that David's got a new contract for a mini-series?'

'That's great. But what about everything else?'

'We're just enjoying what we've got right now.'

I wanted out of the conversation. I felt stifled. She was so horribly young. And so horribly, happily pregnant. I wanted to scream at her: 'You have no idea how it feels to wake up every day with a longing I can't fill, trying not to be jealous of every well-meaning pregnant friend who shares all her maternal stories with me.' But I feigned a smile even over the phone, and assured her that we really weren't that bothered. I don't know if she believed me. What I was sure of was that no-one would know about our next move.

16

I'd always thought of myself as someone who could face her problems head-on and who could deal with them in practical ways. But I'd never really faced a problem like this one. Having discreetly graduated from the "getting pregnant" forum on *Babyworld* to the "infertility" one, I was trying to come to terms with the possibility of real failure. Yet most of the time I continued to tell myself that it was just a slow process for us, that it would take time. And, in any case, some months just couldn't be counted. Like the one when I was away on business and the one when I'd crashed the car. I had started charting my ovulation again, using a computer programme to do it this time, dotting when we made love and when I was likely to be "peaking" in my cycle. Some women swear by this; perhaps for them it's just a way of trying to stay sane. It nearly made me insane. I wasn't a woman any more, but a graph. "Today" or "not yet" became code for our most intimate sexual encounters.

We'd tried to talk about everything, but after a year I'd stopped giving David updates on my internal movements, because I didn't want him to get all excited about nothing. That had made things worse. He was afraid to ask me how I was feeling, whether I thought I was pregnant. He didn't know if I was doing tests on the sly. I'd started to shut him out and we were both getting a bit lonely again. We eventually had that talk.

'This isn't going to work, is it?'

'No, we're driving ourselves mad.'

'I know. What are we doing?'

'I love you so much. We'll be OK. And anyway, it's early days yet.'

'Sort of. But I think we should see someone now.'

'Are you sure you're up to it?'

'Yes, if you are. I'll make a call tomorrow.'

David's face visibly relaxed. He told me later how he'd been treading on eggshells in those few months. He said he felt impotent, in every sense. He tried not to look around him, in the street, in the car park, in the supermarket. He tried not to compare himself with other men. Especially those men he watched playing with, yelling at, or even ignoring, their own children. He was trying not to focus on the word "dad", and feigning casual disinterest in the role of man-as-father, just as I was doing with motherhood. It hurt him, too, to be asked if he had any kids. It was time to take action.

The doctor was young and sympathetic, talked to us for about half an hour, gave us general advice and suggested that we get some tests done, to "be on the safe side". She asked about our sexual and family histories, told David to steer clear of hot baths and tight underwear and booked me in for an internal examination with her and for blood tests at the hospital. Meanwhile, David was off to a clinic for tests of his own. I went for my internal exam and she couldn't find anything immediately wrong. I then dutifully headed off to the hospital and they took five lots of blood from me. Maybe, I was told, you have endometriosis. At the clinic, David had to give a fresh sample. He didn't like it. But nor did he like the fact that I was the one having needles jabbed into me.

We returned to our alcohol-free regime from Monday to Friday, drank very little caffeine, did no excessive exercise and lived as "stress-free" as we could. Except for the huge stress of not being able to have a baby. I bought an American Indian smudge stick to waft over my body every night, but David choked on the fumes and thought I'd gone mad, so I had to throw it away.

Eventually we received a bamboozling set of results. The doctor told me that I seemed to be normal, whatever that means. When David called for his results from our friendly female doctor we found that she had caved in to the difficulties of working in the Health Service and had left. So a terse, patrician male colleague told David just to 'keep trying'. David wanted clarification. Was he normal? Of course he was normal. He had dinner ready for me when I got home and I could sense his relief as he told me his results. We were both "normal" and our infertility remained unexplained. All we could do was to keep trying.

Maybe I was just stuck in the middle of someone else's nightmare. I could never really believe that the problems I was explaining to doctors and nurses were my own. PMT haunted me badly in those days, too, as if to emphasise my predicament. We had talked about IVF treatment as a medium- to long-term possibility during our meeting with the doctor. But we had both decided that it would not be for us. Too many chemicals and unknown side effects. Not a "natural" way to have a baby. Going down the IVF route would, we thought, confirm once and for all that we really had a "problem" and needed advanced medical technology for help. Instead, we had begun to entertain the notion of adoption. Just the merest possibility. My fear was that the adoption agency would probably tell us that we were too old. The real motive for considering adoption at that time, though, was a strangely paradoxical one: we had heard that many couples adopt and then, as a consequence of no longer panicking about having a baby of their own, get pregnant after all. In some ways, then, we were seeing adoption as an alternative to IVF. But none of these thoughts were properly formulated in our minds. We were ill informed and still consumed by a desire for our own baby.

After thirteen months of trying to conceive a baby, David received the letter. Our initial GP had taken a look at his sperm results and was not as sanguine about them as her elderly male colleague. Apparently, he had only looked at count, not at other factors such as motility and morphology. And it was the latter which gave her cause for concern. David walked through the hall and into the kitchen with the open letter in his hand. He had turned very pale and suddenly looked haggard. It was, he said, his fault after all. It's very difficult to try to reassure your partner that nobody is at fault when you know that you would feel the same. From the start, I'd expected my bad periods to be the symptom of a deeper problem. David, almost unknowingly, had also talked in those terms at the beginning, trying to reassure me that it didn't matter, that we'd deal with it together. The implicit suggestion that it is a woman's problem has a long historical heritage. David had been so understanding, so sympathetic. He was great at being the support. Now, though, he took on the blame. I thought he would never get over that letter. He went back for three more consecutive tests. Waiting for the results was dreadful. He would pace up and down before dinner. He would wonder about his family history. He was angry with himself, apart from anything, for not having entertained the real possibility that he might be the one with a problem. But finally we got the results. His level was not great, but falling within the lower end of the "OK" spectrum for the percentage of sperm that are not deformed. The consultant said that he wasn't that worried about the results, that his little swimmers all moved about a lot and were sufficiently numerous. We were both relieved, but determined to help his poor little blighters by giving them all the assistance they might need. We stopped to buy more zinc and some selenium tablets. It was a lesson in how not to apportion blame or cause. We were a couple and had a joint problem to face, as a couple. And that was the end, and beginning, of the story.

But in that same month I received another major blow, and was confirmed in my suspicion that I'm not a very nice person. A close friend who'd emigrated to Australia the previous year told me not only that she was pregnant, but that she was, in fact, six months pregnant. I started to shiver as I read the email and couldn't even finish it. I slammed the lid down on my laptop, grabbed my bag and headed for the gym. I couldn't decide, even by the end of a hard aerobics class, whether I was more resentful of her being pregnant or of her not telling me. Both, I supposed.

I went along to Shaheen, the reflexologist, the following day and she expressed her concern that problems with my uterus kept showing up in my pulses. I was becoming convinced that there was something wrong with me and that I needed to get it fixed. As an anniversary present to us, I called the doctor again and two days later, after examining me thoroughly, she referred me to a gynaecologist and starting muttering about a laparoscopy. A little knowledge is a very bad thing, and that evening spent on the internet persuaded me that I should do everything I could to get out of having a laparoscopy.

A few weeks later, I pulled a muscle in my leg at the gym and went to see a physiotherapist. Lying on the couch, I told her far more than I'd intended. Somehow I knew she understood. In fact, she'd tried and tried for her own baby, only to get pregnant and lose the baby at birth. I felt humbled. She told me she could see the tension and pain in my face – was it that obvious? – and said we needed to relax if we wanted a baby. I got home, put away our remaining tester kits and slung my folic acid tablets in the bin (although I dug them out about two hours later). I even had a strong cup of coffee to celebrate my liberation. It tasted delicious.

When you're obsessing over something, as we self-confessedly were doing, it's important to find distractions. We found the best diversion of all: we decided to move house. Instead of spending evenings thinking about baby names or what to do if we decided to adopt, we began spending our spare time looking for houses on the internet and putting our own up for sale there too. We took splendid photos and uploaded them onto a dedicated house-selling site. We found several houses to look at and would meet in villages after work to look at potential properties. We were making a big-time move out into the countryside. Of course, the plan went awry. We found a far-too-expensive converted seventeenth-century barn. It had a long, sweeping drive down to the L-shaped orange-bricked building and sat in half an acre of lush grounds, with its own extensive vegetable garden and small wood. It was more than we could afford, but the family wanted to sell it quickly. Mother had died and the sale was the children's way to raise cash. I walked around the garden, entertaining the possibility that our own children might be running around the lawns some day. The lounge had an oval window that opened onto the lawn and patio like the entrance to a magic kingdom. We both loved the house and were willing to go for broke over it. I couldn't help feeling optimistic at the possibility of "new house, new baby". The bad news came when David was away for a couple of days doing research. The surveyor called and asked me where I wanted him to start. With the damp? The electrics? The roof or flooring? The risk of subsidence or the flooding? The deal was off unless we wanted to add the value of the house again to make it habitable. I sat at home alone, thinking about the key dates David was missing, and moping.

Soon after that, we found ourselves discussing neither a baby nor a house, but a wedding, set in the idyllic grounds of a converted castle. But, even there we couldn't escape as the priest pronounced that God would bless the happy couple with babies. What does this God say to us? Have we done something wrong? Picking up a newspaper on the way home didn't help, as articles abounded about the pros and cons of funding IVF treatment. For a few days it was in the news all the time. We were already consumed by the topic, but to hear it talked about on the radio or even in the local post office seemed strange. I overheard a woman who was buying stamps and talking to the shopkeeper:

'It's not natural though, is it?' The owner wasn't going to be drawn in, and muttered incoherently in response.

'I mean, a baby from a test tube is like a Frankenstein experiment. That's not what God meant us to do. People who can't have children should just accept it.'

She went on, and on. I wished at that moment that I could be a witch for a day. I'd turn her into a frog. I replaced the paper I was about to buy and escaped from the shop.

When I read newspaper articles, I was impressed at how open some people are about infertility. We had told nobody except our parents and our closest friends. We didn't want people probing into our health or our sex life. Or feeling sorry for us. That would be even worse. The problem is that it's natural and acceptable to ask a person whether they have children, or if they plan to have them. Even house hunting, we found that estate agents were obsessed with the proximity of every house to a "good" school.

'We are too old for school, thanks,' we'd joke. I was starting to feel so old that I felt like saying, 'Our children are grown up and live away'.

The IVF option remained on our table. For a while, I was encouraged by a virtual "friend" I'd encountered on one of the many websites I now secretly inhabited. She'd been "sniffing" and "injecting" and "over-stimulating" and was making the whole treatment of IVF seem very straightforward. She even thought that the drugs made her cheerful. I was starting to be taken in by the idea of this simple procedure. Until, that is, my friend had her first traumatic moments. She'd been sailing along, almost mechanically, but as she injected herself one evening she was suddenly overcome by the enormity of what she was doing: trying to make a baby. She hit a downward spiral and became very tearful and depressed for a couple of weeks. I was no longer sure that we'd be up to it. But part of me wondered if we had much choice.

David would still have preferred to say nothing to anyone. But I was finding it hard not to be able to talk about it. My mother was too emotional and David had heard it all over and over again and had to live with it every day. He agreed that it would be fine to mention it to a few people, though without making a great big thing of it and getting all upset in the process. So we were quite matter-of-fact in telling my old school friend Jill and her husband Pete. Jill partly comprehended; after all, she'd had to try for six months for her second longed-for baby. But Pete was almost peacock-like, asserting his lack of understanding by saying that he'd never had any problems getting women pregnant, in his first marriage or his second. It was sickening. We'd shared a secret and wished we hadn't. It wasn't really his fault, but it was insulting. Pete was point-scoring and playing that horrible male game, which makes the infertility question so hard for men in the first place. My need to talk diminished immediately and we went back to keeping our secret.

One of our coping mechanisms was to stay busy. I think I'd have gone mad without a full-time job in those months. My teaching schedule was jam-packed and I offered after-college tuition and other study groups on top of that. We went out to hear a lot of jazz and visited the cinema and theatre more often. We felt that we were clawing back our real lives and that it was important to put the baby issue – central as it was – into a more manageable place. Most impressively, we continued to pursue our house-buying adventure. Having lost our dream barn, we'd found a small house in a large garden on the edge of town. The house needed some major renovation as its very kind owner had lived there for over fifty years, and apparently done no decorating during that time. We put in an offer and it was accepted. But the following morning we received a call to let us know that our own buyers were pulling out, and the inevitable collapse happened. Our house had been on the market for four months, and we were almost £1,000 out of pocket with nothing to show for it.

We viewed over thirty houses during the following six weeks and kept a steady trickle of would-be buyers coming through our own front door. Eventually, we had a bite from a family who offered us more or less the asking price. We had to find somewhere now, so went to our "emergency" list. One house was in the middle of a farm – they hadn't mentioned that; another had a railway running through the back garden – and they hadn't mentioned that; a third had a complicated cess-pit system – they hadn't mentioned that either; and yet another was set in what can only be described as a dog's toilet – a fact which had also been omitted from the further particulars. We were getting nowhere, but at least our frustrations were channelled in a new direction. We were on the point of giving up when we decided to go and see two more houses on the day of our new buyers' ultimatum. The first was hopeless: dark throughout, it had strangely shaped rooms and was decorated atrociously everywhere. It was also well above our price range. We departed after two minutes and thought about cancelling our last viewing and going straight to the pub. But as it was on the way home, and as we didn't want to be rude to the owners who were now expecting us, we went anyway. We slowly pulled up outside a dormer bungalow that looked as though an old lady had lived in it for a long time, except for the fact that the driveway was full of cars and vans.

'Oh well, this will only take two minutes,' I thought. The hallway was long and thin, like a hotel corridor with lots of rooms off to each side. But although decorated with green floral patterns and pink carpets, the inside felt like a family home. The word "family" shot into my head and stayed there. Walking into the huge dining kitchen, I knew that this was a happy house, but when we entered the light-filled lounge and looked out onto the back garden, we both instantly fell in love with the whole place. We wanted it, and within half a mile of leaving I called the estate agents from my mobile to put in an offer. Before we got home our offer had been accepted. We called our buyers in the nick of time and saved our own house sale. This was a major bit of luck and we felt fantastic. At last, we had something positive to show from our baby trials. We took my parents to visit the house the following day and loved it even more than we had on our first viewing. We spent about an hour just wandering around the sprawling garden: it was desolate, leaf-strewn and bare, but we adored it. Within one-and-a-half more cycles of trying to make a family, we were unpacking boxes in our new house.

Despite the happy move, Christmas returned to haunt us and I really struggled to keep it together. We should have booked a holiday to somewhere hot and romantic. Instead, we sat through an excruciating family dinner, trying not to say what we were thinking and just wanting to run away. We had managed to control the baby cravings during the frenzied house-buying months, but now they attacked us again with a vengeance. One morning I got up to find that I was bleeding. I was early, again. As I shuffled, head down and miserable, into the bathroom, I felt a heat rise in my chest. I felt as though an alien being possessed me, and it was strangling me from the inside. My face was on fire, I could feel tears welling up and stinging my eyes, and I couldn't breathe properly. My breath came in gasps, short, sharp and panicked. David had just rolled out of bed and was sauntering in to brush his teeth when he heard me wheezing. He looked terrified, but ran over and put his hands on my shoulders. Looking me in the face, he made me moderate my breathing with his, take full deep breaths and let them out very slowly. I calmed down quickly, but he sat with me and put my head between my legs and a cold, wet flannel on the back of my neck. This had never happened to me before. I was frightened but felt eerily calm. I called Shaheen and told her what had happened. She told me that it sounded like a panic attack. When I saw her that afternoon, she gave me some great breathing techniques to try out and I had a full body massage to remove all the tension. I felt exhilarated afterwards and booked for a follow-up appointment three days later.

Shaheen kept saying how she'd always wanted to treat a woman throughout labour and childbirth. I told her that if I ever did become pregnant, she wouldn't be allowed to go on holiday when I was due to give birth. We were birthing buddies, without any prospect of a birth. In the meantime, Shaheen had been doing some investigating of her own and suggested that I went to her acupuncturist friend, Tamsin.

She was convinced that she could get to the root of our problem more quickly and told me how she'd already discussed my case with her friend. Luckily for us, Tamsin had a free appointment the following evening. David wasn't that keen to go, so I went to the local complementary health centre by myself. By now, we were overdosing on complementary therapies and David was starting to become a firm non-believer. So, he said, was his wallet.

Tamsin was dark-haired and mysterious and looked half-Egyptian. She greeted me with the glistening smile of a dental hygienist and almost hugged me. She led me upstairs to a treatment room painted in soothing cream and gentle orange. The preliminary talk lasted for over an hour and I felt as though I was in therapy. Finally, she asked me to take off most of my clothes and lie down on the bench. I reflected on how far I'd come in overcoming my prudish tendencies. Her hand was warm as she took my pulses. She said she could feel some unevenness in my stomach and abdominal area and that my tongue – which I'd been forced to expose to her – was damp. Wasn't my tongue supposed to be damp? Apparently not. She then gave me needles and mox. Mox is like having little incense pyramids placed on your body and burned down. I was convinced that they would burn down to my skin, but she always stopped them in time, so I began to relax. Towards the end of the session she began to cough. And cough. And cough some more. She explained that sometimes this happened to her; she was taking in all my problems. She looked pretty dreadful and exhausted by the time she'd finished, but I felt great. She went home to shower off the effects of treating me; I went home to the best night's sleep I'd had in a long time. I was eager to have more sessions.

Meanwhile, I went back to Shaheen for my follow-up, only to come out feeling more emotionally overwrought than when I went in. Shaheen told me that she was going to have her own, unplanned, baby. She had her problems to deal with, but they were not ones I wanted to imagine at that moment. I just kept wondering if her feet were now puffy. Having smiled my fake congratulations, I got in the car vowing never to see her again. And I didn't.

Towards the end of my second treatment with Tamsin, she put a needle in my chest and I started to weep. I controlled myself quickly, but it had come out of nowhere. She said that such a reaction wasn't uncommon. She also, rather mysteriously, said that we often find things we're not looking for with these kinds of treatments. She told me how one woman had gone to her with fertility issues but during the course of treatment decided that she didn't actually want to be with her husband any more. I hoped that she wouldn't uncover anything quite so drastic in my case. Unfortunately, that wasn't the only time she made me cry. After about four months of visiting her, Tamsin told me that she was rebalancing my blood flow and calming my pre-menstrual tummy. I could not remember feeling quite so relaxed for a long time. She told me to get dressed, but then returned unusually quickly. She looked uncomfortable and spoke hesitantly:

'I don't want to upset you, Laurel, but feel that you should know . . . It will be obvious soon enough anyway.' She paused some more and I refused to make it any easier for her.

'I'm pregnant.'

I fought off the stunned silence that overcame me to stutter my congratulations. I felt as if someone had knocked me over. Somehow I felt betrayed. It was totally irrational, but I couldn't help myself. I forced a smile and turned away, stumbled over to the chair in the corner and towards the clothes I'd casually, and happily, draped over it. I dropped my watch and fumbled for it in my shoes.

'Are you OK?' She sounded genuinely concerned.

'Yes, of course. I'm really happy for you. When's the baby due?'

I didn't even hear the answer. Instead, I grimaced

inwardly when she tried too hard to deflect the situation by telling me she'd have to work on me now, so that I too could be pregnant. I felt dizzy as I bent down to get the shopping I'd left on the floor, and she caught my arm. I told her I was fine, that it was only the treatment. I just wanted to talk my way out of the building. I paid her hastily and booked another appointment, knowing full well that I would never come for it. I'd cancel it later, but I didn't want Tamsin to know how much I was hurting. I fled to my car as quickly as I could and sobbed uncontrollably for the ten-minute ride home. First my reflexologist and now the acupuncturist. Maybe the chi was flowing in the wrong direction. Why did it seem wrong that they should be able to conceive? Was it because I thought they really understood my situation, but realized now that they never could?

We tried a couple of other complementary routes. I even dragged David to a pilates-style class full of women of a certain age. He was the only man. In fact, I think he was the only man ever to have attended. The class was one of those where people looking in from the outside mumble knowingly about the "lightweight", "easy", "call that exercise?" moves going on inside. But once you are twisting your head through your legs, or trying to lift yourself onto your hands from a squatting position, you are quickly drenched with sweat. We gave the class up after two sessions. We even went to see a healer at Tamsin's centre. He simply told me that he felt a lovely light energy field around me, but didn't say what it might mean. David apparently caused this man's hands to feel burning. But as he didn't seem to have a clue what this might indicate, we gave up on that option, too.

Whilst I had been getting to know Tamsin, she'd recommended a friend of hers who specialised in Chinese herbal medicine, as well as acupuncture. When I gave up on Tamsin, we decided to give him a go. At least he couldn't get pregnant, although with my record I did wonder. This time it was David's turn to be the guinea pig. He made an appointment, and one mid-week evening arrived at a grey-fronted block of 1960s flats. He told me later how his knock on the door produced a fresh-faced college type. It isn't only the policemen who are getting younger all the time, he thought. He was taken upstairs to a small treatment room. It had Chinese pictures and calligraphy on the walls and a long treatment table dominated the centre of the room. David was ready to jump onto it, but Ted beckoned him to a schoolroom chair in a corner, where he sat opposite David and took copious notes as they talked for over an hour. David was getting used to expressing himself, to being open about his problems and honest about his expectations, but he still didn't like it and certainly didn't feel the need to unburden himself. Eventually, Ted took pulses, walked round David several times, examined his tongue and reflected for a minute or two, before deciding to try out a few needles. As he did so, he talked positively about the value of acupuncture and herbs on male fertility. He was almost certain that we could overcome it, but did qualify his claim by saying that I would need to be treated too. He also promised to concoct a special potion of Chinese herbs for David to take every morning.

When he arrived home, David was exhausted and had to have an early night. Maybe acupuncture mixed with herbs wasn't going to be so good for our baby project after all. Despite this, he was buoyed by Ted's sheer optimism and was determined to maximise our chances. Inevitably, it wasn't long before Ted explained how he'd be away for paternity leave for a couple of weeks. But either I was growing immune to the pain of hearing other people's birth stories, or else I felt sufficiently removed from the mother-to-be this time. I had also started visiting his clinic every month, and he'd miraculously eased my periods with his needles and potions. The only problem with the latter was the pestilential smell and taste. Even the cats stopped hovering for extra food when we were mixing them. For the next few months, Ted would mix and match our acupuncture and herbal remedies and we would drink our magic potions. In fact, my period pains did lessen, but so did my enthusiasm for going to see Ted. We'd tried it all: reflexology, acupuncture, Chinese herbs, healing and candles. Reluctant as we were, it was time to give Western medical science a go.

My thirty-fifth birthday was drawing near and my consciousness of not being a mother was heightened to the point of agony. This is definitely not how I thought it would be. David's thirty-fifth birthday would come only two weeks after mine. Our joint treat was booking an appointment to see the consultant privately. After our last visit to the doctor we'd been put on the NHS waiting list and told to expect to wait up to twenty-one weeks. For £135 we could have our first consultation within two weeks. Not quite the present either of us had really wanted. Then, in a process that would turn out to be smooth sailing all the way until the end, the NHS appointment suddenly arrived. We duly cancelled the private appointment. We could move one step forwards. We were excited, very excited indeed, and felt as though we were doing something: we were temporarily back in control.

3

'So what's next?'

By this time, our life no longer ran in calendar months, but in cycles. If I had to make an appointment with the doctor, hairdresser or dentist, I would think: 'How many chances do I have for a baby before my next visit?' There was an advert on the radio about a woman attending a job interview. She was consumed with the thought that she might be pregnant and unintended baby-related words and phrases would slip out during her answers. It was an advert for a pregnancy tester kit, although why the company needed to advertise now that it had me as a customer, I didn't understand.

Moving into the new house had been wonderful. I'd had to focus on the move, worry about the cats, give a paper at a conference, and host a flurry of guests. None of them knew, apart from Mum and Dad. The house and garden would make an ideal family home – so the estate agent had said. Now we just had to make the ideal family. We had both secretly hoped for a new-house-new-baby miracle to happen. But it hadn't, and with the move behind us, we were focusing on the one project we still had to complete.

Too much of our existence depended on pretence, covering up, as if we were ashamed of what we saw to be the biggest failure of our lives. Our pretence was so good that our new neighbours assumed that we disliked children. We wanted to shout: 'We love children and just wish we had some of our own,' but at the same time didn't want to be drafted in as babysitters too soon. With the New Year out of the way, we'd quietly gone about the business of redecorating and setting up a family home, for whatever family we would eventually become.

The village school had a painted red smiley face on its front wall and we would often pass the sound of cheering children in the playground. Would our child ever go there? I would chastise myself for even thinking it, but would then indulge the fantasy of picking up my daughter from the gates. I suppose for some parents that is a chore; for me, it seemed more like a beautiful dream.

When my mum's birthday came round again, I remembered how much I'd dreamt of telling her our good news the year before. Once again, though, I could only hand over a brightly wrapped small box with a dull present inside.

As it turned out, it was the initial announcement by Jane and Andrew, David's younger brother, and not the arrival of their beautiful baby girl, that hurt the most. When Monica was finally born, we practically ram-raided Mothercare and got hooked on Ebay. We collected one of every little thing and a number of larger presents, from a real sponge to a giant green toy dog and mobile-covered play mat. I wrapped each one carefully and put them all in a giant box that would barely fit into the car. Monica was unimpressed; she just lay asleep in David's arms. But Andrew and Jane were touched at our thoughtfulness and I felt remarkably calm. David sat there happily holding his niece. It didn't hurt. Perhaps because we were being nice. Because we felt good about being generous. Because we were doing something practical, not moping. Monica wasn't ours, would never be ours, but she was part of our story.

Our story, we were discovering, was the story of

hundreds, if not thousands, of others in this country and elsewhere. Lurking in the grey shadows of social inadequacy, featuring in the occasional, marginal newspaper column or the one-off interview on *Women's Hour*: they want better NHS treatment, but don't want anybody to know about it. And so I continued to hover on *Babyworld*, assumed a false identity and reinvented myself over and over again. Only the problems I discussed were real: how does one begin adoption proceedings? Are there any herbal treatments to energise reluctant sperm and eggs? What colour should cervical mucus be during the middle of my cycle? These were people, mostly women, with whom to share my worries. One day I discovered a woman who was having tests at the same hospital that I would soon be visiting regularly. We agreed to chat on the phone and compare notes. Her name, online at least, was Rachel. She had been trying to have a baby for over ten years, had lost two in early miscarriages and one at birth, and went on having numerous tests. Her body seemed to reject the idea of a baby. What struck me was her positive attitude.

'I'm just going to keep trying. We still have lots of options open, including ICSI.'

ICSI, she explained, stands for intracytoplasmic sperm injection and means, in effect, that the egg is collected from the woman before being injected directly with a single sperm. The resulting embryo is then transferred to the woman's womb. It differs from in-vitro fertilisation (IVF), which requires the egg to be taken from the woman and placed in a Petri dish containing the man's sperm for fertilisation there. If all goes to plan, a sperm fuses with the egg to form a single cell (called a zygote, which sounds more like something out of *Doctor Who*), which then starts dividing and becomes an embryo. This is transferred to the woman's womb and, if it implants successfully, develops as a normal embryo. This is the unromantic reality for the almost one in six couples that now have difficulty conceiving.

'So, what's next?'

'We're going for our preliminary ICSI appointment next month. And we'll take it from there.'

'Aren't you worried about it? The drugs, potential side effects, the pressure?'

'I know what it's like to carry a growing baby inside, to feel it developing. When Adam was born, it was already too late; he'd stopped breathing inside me. But I still loved him so much; the bond was already strong between us. I know he's in heaven now, helping me get through this, so that we can make a brother or sister for him. I can't let him down and it's all we want.'

I didn't know what else to say, but felt that my own troubles were still quite small compared to Rachel's.

The following week was a case of very bad timing. One of my younger students asked to see me. Looking confident and determined, she explained to me in a very matter-of-fact tone that she wouldn't be able to hand in her work on time as she was going to have an abortion and would have to take a few days off. I felt as though I was suffocating and needed to get out into the fresh air. I made the excuse of going to fetch the relevant form and rushed out of my office and the building. I wasn't judging her; it was her life and her decision. But it seemed so unfair to me. Perhaps in some ways we were in the same position: society either frowned upon us or didn't understand us.

Less than three weeks later I got the call from Rachel. She'd had an excruciating two-week wait after the implants, had had severe cramps and started to bleed a little. She had been ready for the worst news.

'I can't believe it, Laurel, but I'm pregnant.'

I felt an overwhelming sense of joy and even surprised myself. I'd expected to have at least a twinge of jealousy. But she'd been through so much, much more than I had. And it had paid off.

'I still keep skipping round the house and singing. Of course, we have a long way to go and things could go wrong, but this is the start we've prayed for. It would be great to think you were right behind me.'

When I put down the phone I decided that David and I should go through all the pros and cons of IVF after all. Think about it carefully and rule it in or out once and for all. If we were honest, we had more or less become resigned to the fact that we wouldn't conceive naturally. But I still wasn't sure that IVF was for us. What do you say to your seven-year-old daughter when she asks where she comes from? How do teenagers, with their existing angst, go through schooldays knowing that they came from a test tube? But how else could we have a baby of our own?

A few weeks later, I was at work exchanging pleasantries with an office assistant from the floor below. She announced proudly that her newly-wed daughter was pregnant, and before I could stop myself, I said:

'Good grief, already?' Dana was offended.

'She's already been married for three months,' she countered.

Of course. In her eyes I must be a freak, I thought. I reached my office as my telephone began to ring. I fumbled with my keys, unlocked the door and grabbed the receiver just before the answerphone kicked in. It was Rachel, barely comprehensible.

'What on earth is the matter?'

'Come now, please, help me.'

When I got to Rachel's I knew straightaway that she'd lost the baby. Steve was already getting the car ready to take her to hospital. I hugged her and helped her down the front path. She looked like a ghost.

That evening I visited Rachel in hospital. Steve had gone for something to eat.

'How do you feel?'

'Dead. How can I say goodbye to this baby too?'

I was crying, but she had no tears left. Looking at Rachel, I thought I knew what "tired of life" meant.

At that moment the doctor came in and I was asked to

let Rachel rest. I wondered if she could ever rest again.

In spite of Rachel's experience, we headed into a process we'd always agreed we would avoid. Artificial insemination. Test-tube babies. All of the terms are as cold and uncomfortable as the process itself and seem to remove nature from the heart of the most natural experience of childbirth. The most important part of our headlong drive into treatment was the proactive nature of it. We were doing something. And, good or bad, it could only move us forward, help us to tick a few more boxes of "things to do". We had more blood tests. And we drove to the hospital, which was a building site, and would be until our baby was old enough to go to nursery school. We eventually fought our way into a car parking space, avoiding the diggers and lorries all around. David had had the same problem three days earlier when he had been to give yet another sample. The fertility treatment department was intentionally situated in its own bungalow-style building on the outskirts of the main hospital. After all, we were not ill. As soon as we walked into the blue-carpeted entrance, we were welcomed by a smiling receptionist and ushered to comfortable red chairs in the middle of the room. It was not intimidating. It did not smell of hospitals. We felt calm, but David still squeezed my hand tightly from time to time. Suddenly he squeezed it very hard and steered me to a seat out of the way in one dark corner. He motioned with his eyes towards a couple. I recognised them at once, but didn't know where from.

'The post office in town,' whispered David.

As far as we knew, this couple smiled every day at people collecting money, stamps and driving licences. And yet, all the time, just like us, they were struggling with infertility. You never know what is going on behind the smile of the person next to you. For no logical reason, we were embarrassed.

After about ten minutes a nurse came out to call us. The three couples before us had already gone through. Her crisp and clean blue uniform made the only noise as we walked down a narrow corridor to a treatment room. We sat on orange plastic chairs and she took down all our personal details. We were soon joined by a registrar, who sat and talked us through the implications of all our results. Blood tests. Semen tests. Thankfully, she treated us as intelligent individuals. I don't think I could have coped with being patronised at that moment. My results, apparently, were all normal – whatever normal means when the whole process of conception is really just the random collision of cells. David's latest news was that he too was still normal. We were, apparently, in the popular category of "unexplained infertility" and were presented with two options by Mr Price, the diminutive and quietly spoken consultant: IUI (intra-uterine injection) or ICSI, as Rachel had had. The first is like squirting sperm into a bottle with an egg and shaking it all about. As far as he was concerned, ICSI would be the better option. So we agreed there and then to give it a go. Perhaps we should have gone home to talk about it, but there comes a point when you feel you've done far too much talking already. Luckily for us, we just fitted their criteria to obtain NHS funding, saving us £2,200. So here we were, after forever renouncing the idea of IVF, about to start our own course of treatment. We were told that the approval for funding was likely to take up to six months. After that, it could possibly take another three months to get the process started. In the meantime, I was to go for another set of blood tests and a pelvic scan. Could I be pregnant by this time next year? We felt excited and optimistic and left hospital saying very little to one another. As a treat, and because we'd been too nervous to have lunch, we went into town for a cream tea at a cosy café. We had a chance to have a baby after all and, we thought, we might even conceive whilst we're waiting. David was a bit quiet for the rest of the afternoon.

'Are you OK? I thought you were pleased.'

'I am, but, well, the treatment sounds rather painful and

you have to have it all. That doesn't seem fair.'

'It's not as if you're pushing me into anything, is it? This is a small price to pay if we can really have a baby. Surely a bit of discomfort and a few drugs would be worth it?'

'As long as you're sure. You know you can pull out of the treatment any time you want.'

'Don't worry; I'll certainly play on your guilt. Red roses and some Swiss chocolate should keep me going.'

'You do know, don't you, that at the end of the day I don't care about anything except you.'

That was all I needed to know.

I had an assessment scan at the clinic and was introduced on the scan to several ripening follicles. In a way, that day was the start of our ICSI process. And from that moment, it all happened much more quickly than expected. Even though our funding hadn't been approved, we went for an information session and they took blood from a whimpering David and also from me. It was a shock to realise just how soon we might become parents, after all this time. While we were in the waiting zone, I realised that we'd only had sex once during the key dates for that month. David had been away on a trip and when he returned I was full of 'flu. But how amazing, I thought, that I'd not calculated it as a big deal. As I mused about this with David one Saturday morning over breakfast, the post thudded into the hallway. An innocuous white envelope hid the exciting news that our funding had been approved. We were in shock. We had agreed to give ourselves more time to conceive by ourselves, but with this opportunity now right in front of us, we were suddenly desperate to get on with the treatment. I called the clinic immediately but they didn't return the call until Monday morning. I could hardly sleep on Sunday. The nurse called at nine and suggested that I start straightaway. Gulp. I could go for a swab two days later and be "sniffing" drugs within the week. We were both painfully excited.

In my excitement I had forgotten about the possible

pain. The swab hurt quite a lot. Ridiculously, I felt underlying panic. What if, by some miracle, I was already pregnant? Then I'd be giving my baby all these drugs. You're not supposed to have unprotected sex in the month you start treatment, but we'd had no idea that it would begin so soon. That thought didn't stop me from grinning a lot when I went to pick up my huge bag of drugs from the hospital pharmacy. Funding covers the cost of the drugs, but the prescription itself still cost £25. How do some people afford this? As she handed me my bag of goodies, the pharmacist wished me good luck. Right at that moment, I felt fantastic. After one week of "sniffing" drugs aimed at calming my system down, I didn't feel any different. David even said that I was looking great. Apart from the taste – like eye drops that drip into the back of your throat – I apparently had no side effects. No beard or deep voice. If it all worked out, I realised, I would have about thirty-seven days to go until I knew.

I did have one absolutely humungous tantrum. David had asked his parents to be discreet, but they had told his brother and his wife, who then left a phone message to wish us good luck. How nice. I was irate and tossed my slippers down the stairs, narrowly missing the right ear of my panic-stricken husband. I swore more in two minutes than I have ever sworn in my life. I'd been pretending that I was totally fine and practical about ICSI, about taking hormonal drugs and about not being able to conceive without them. But deep down I was actually terrified: of the drugs, of the possible side effects, of having to inject myself soon. Most of all, though, I was scared about the possibility of failure. I'd never really wanted to keep something to myself so much. Without a busy job and life to keep me occupied, I'd have been on my way to a mental institution. Despite my blip, the sniffing went on and I had a baseline scan. The consultant told me that my now empty ovaries were ready for the next stage and patted me on the leg as he left. This meant that injections loomed. But the "gun" made the whole process easy and I soon settled into the new routine. It didn't really hurt, either, although David turned white the couple of times he watched.

I couldn't work properly and was totally distracted by thoughts of babies. After ten injections, I had a constant gentle ache in my ovaries, but worried that I wasn't in sufficient pain to have golf-ball-sized follicles swimming around down there. When I went for my second scan I met a woman on her second IVF attempt. She seemed chirpy. I was starting to see other familiar faces there. Hannah and Clare were at the same stage as I was. When I came out from my scan Hannah looked as though she was crying. I watched her being led into a private room. I would never see her again. I went to work and tried to get everything done in one day for the whole week. It looked as though David would have to take the day off to take me in. I had to give myself one special timed, big injection and was now ready for the next phase.

I got the go-ahead at the following day's scan. As soon as we entered the clinic, we were taken through to the recovery room. David was very anxious, as I had my blood pressure taken and pulse looked at, signed forms and read information. The registrar came and talked me through the procedure and I was ready to go before I knew it. The operation lasted thirty minutes and they'd collected fourteen eggs. David was worried sick. He'd been asked to leave for twenty minutes while they woke me up, oxygen mask still on my face. And that was it. Sadie, the nurse, said it was time to leave, but as I stood up and started to retch I sat down again and threw up in the bag she handed me. I slept a little more and when I awoke the pain in my stomach was terrible. David drove me home carefully and stayed with me. I slept in bed – so did he, from the exhaustion of worry – all afternoon, before managing a couple of Weetabix for dinner. I got home to online good luck messages from my *Babyworld* friends. No-one else knew. Work had just been told I needed an operation for "women's problems" – men never ask follow-up questions to those kinds of statements. The next day the embryologist called to tell me they'd injected twelve eggs and nine had fertilised. And so all that remained was to have the best two put back inside me and then to wait. The rest could be frozen.

It wasn't long before I started to get bad stomach-ache and deep down I already knew what would come. This was something we just couldn't control. My mum cried when I told her; she was as frustrated as we were. I had a bloody night in every sense, and felt miserable. And it took a few weeks for me to return to normal.

'Laurel, we really need to talk.'

'There isn't anything to talk about, is there? We can't have a baby and the rest of the universe can.'

'Don't be like that, why don't we talk about our options?'

'Options to have more operations or other people's unwanted kids. Sounds perfect.'

'Laurel, please.' I could see the tears in his eyes but I didn't care anymore. 'What do you want me to say?'

'Tell me this is just a nightmare and that we'll wake up from it one day. Why us? It's just not fair.'

'Come on, people have to go through much worse than this.'

'It doesn't feel like that for me right now.'

'I know, I'm sorry and wish I could make it better.'

I didn't disagree with him. I stood up from the table and walked out. He didn't follow me. An hour later I emerged from the bathroom, with puffy eyes and a determined smile. But David wasn't there. He'd left a note on the table. He'd gone to his brother's, for a night off. Something inside me snapped. Never before had I exploded in an instant. I ripped up the papers nearest to me on the table. A couple of unwashed plates were swept onto the floor. They crashed and broke into sharp pieces. The roar inside me subsided and a strange calm replaced it. At that moment a key turned in the front door and I heard David's resigned shuffle in the hallway. As soon as he took in the chaos of the kitchen floor he raced over and held me. After about twenty minutes he loosened his protective grip. I was shivering.

'I think you need some help.' I let him lead me upstairs to a bath and bed.

The next day I thought about what he'd said. Had it really come to that? What kind of help did I need? Help to save our marriage from this trauma, or help to save my mind? It didn't take me long to decide.

'I'm sorry, David. You've had a hell of a couple of days. I've been selfish, self-indulgent. I'm so sorry. I'll be OK, I just need to sort myself out a bit.'

'Does this mean I can start scattering papers again and stop treading on eggshells around you?'

'Yes, please.'

And that was, really, the end of my mini life crisis. For some women, and men, it lasts much longer. Some people need to turn to professional help. I felt better just knowing that I could get it if I really needed it. But at this point I just needed to be with my husband. In the end, we booked a long weekend away in Barcelona and did things that only a couple without children can do so easily. It felt great.

We drew up plans for the garden and we found ways to laugh a lot. With childless friends. At parties. In the cinema. We would give ourselves two more ICSI attempts; we had six frozen embryos to play with. I called the clinic to check out what I would have to do and was very happy to discover that I could go with my own cycle, without drugs or operations and just have the embryos implanted at the right moment of the month. And we even resolved that if those ICSI attempts failed, we would call the adoption services to find out much more. But we both hoped that it wouldn't come to that.

I felt from the start of our second attempt at ICSI that it wasn't going to work: we were using defrosted embryos; I was ready on the Sunday but the implantation would only happen on the Monday; and it really, really, really hurt. My old man wasted no time in shattering the few hopes I'd clung to. As I lay cuddling my hot water bottle in bed, David sat on the edge and we started then to talk about adoption. Just as a vague possibility. Just as a fallback. We needed to believe that we still had options. We had three embryos left (the rest had perished) but I wasn't sure I wanted to go through that again. I was numbed by this second failure, but there were no tears this time. We would pay for the storage of the frozen embryos for the next couple of years, convinced that we wouldn't want to use them but reluctant to have them destroyed.

So, our minds started to focus on Square One: the possibility of adoption. We had tried everything. Six months had passed since the trip to the healer, it was four months since our most recent visit to the acupuncturist, and we'd spent many low-alcohol, high-energy months trying to make our own baby. But after almost two years, and long before many other couples who just keep going, we were ready to concede defeat. At least, that is how we viewed our position at first. After a while, though, and especially after the experience of finding out more about adoption, we came to realise that life was taking us in a new direction. Adoption did not mean the consolation prize.

4

Thinking about adoption

Having abandoned a process we'd been determined not to start in the first place, we found ourselves back where we started. We still hadn't quite given up the hope of making our own baby, but our thoughts now turned seriously towards adoption. Before our long journey towards IVF, I'd called the local authority to ask for advice about how to go about it. The gently spoken woman on the end of the phone was the kind of person I could have unburdened my heart to. But I had remained as calm as possible, sounding as though I was seeking advice rather than help. It soon became clear that one consideration for us would be how little exposure we had to children. We didn't baby-sit. We didn't see our niece very often or have other little people over for weekends with their parents. When they first say that to you, it makes you want to scream. Of course we don't have much exposure to babies, because we can't have any! But once I'd finished muttering about her comments, I accepted grudgingly that they made sense. They have to find the most appropriate adopters. Demand for white newborns far outweighs supply, so we needed to be able to tick as many boxes as possible. Both of us felt as though we'd returned to a place where we should have been; that

IVF had been a painful diversion. It soon became clear that the process of adoption would not be pain-free either, but we decided that this long, intrusive journey might be worth starting. We would be inundated with forms, and have to give intimate details of our life to strangers. But then, hadn't we been doing that for the past couple of years anyway? At least this time there would be no needles and internal examinations. How hard could it be? Maybe, I thought, IVF was meant to be a preparation for us.

The initial stage took absolutely ages: I called, they sent forms, and we filled them in and returned them. We were assigned an initial assessor, but not told her name or details. Three weeks later, Sally called to arrange a home visit. The best she could do was to visit almost three-and-a-half weeks later. We searched websites, read books, and informed ourselves down to the smallest ridiculous detail about adoption. We discussed the "what ifs?" of adoption day and night. At breakfast, 'What if they ask us to take siblings?' That was our "in for a penny" moment, idealising the joy of having a child – and therefore why not two?

We scrubbed the house clean and banished the cats in preparation for Sally's visit. I bought a huge bunch of pink lilies and David timed the coffee maker to come on at the perfect moment. We felt as though we were trying to sell the house. It was a glorious spring afternoon, the sun was streaming through the freshly polished lounge windows and our garden looked magnificent. How could anyone fail to be impressed by our idyllic lifestyle and what we evidently had to offer?

We showered and dressed neatly, casual but not too smart. And waited. Eventually, thirty minutes before she was due to arrive, Sally called to say that she had an urgent case and would not be able to come. Could we reschedule for the following week, same time? The journey from her office to our house was an hour, and yet she'd called only thirty minutes before the appointment. What kind of sloppy, unprofessional outfit were they running? Or was this a test, to see how flexible we are as individuals and with our time? Are we patient and understanding? No. I was angry and upset, and burst into tears, hugging my cup of freshly brewed coffee.

One week later Sally turned up in a 1970s-style bright orange dress with clashing red finger and toenail varnish. This time we couldn't be bothered with the house tidying and it was raining so hard that the garden looked like a dangerous swamp. No apologies for the previous week. We said nothing about it, but we had done our homework. We anticipated every question: the pond issue, the lack of contact with kids issue, the age issue, the job issue, the identity issue, the ethnicity issue, the discipline and behaviour issues. Sally was happy to tick the boxes for us. However, she was sent, apparently, to ensure that we were not still "grieving" about IVF failures and infertility. What a stupid idea. I would never lose this sadness, this deep regret. But I was learning to live with it; we both were.

Sally outlined the process of adoption and we were left thinking there were so many hoops to jump through that if we adopted by the time we were seventy-five we'd be doing well. Also, she told us that the chances of getting a young baby are very slim. We convinced her that we'd be prepared to wait. Before she left, she said she'd try and get us on the required introductory course for February – six months away – and we just nodded, in that resigned way that only couples who've been through IVF can understand. More waiting. Worse, we wouldn't even be told until December whether or not we'd got a place on the course. We moped for a while, walked round the garden and tried not to resent anyone who had ever had a baby. I lay awake that night pondering my desire to become a mother, wondering whether it had actually become a challenge to overcome (I can do it) rather than a desire deep inside. The two things had become mixed up in me.

The following weekend David stopped sipping his tea

and lowered the local paper he was reading. An article on voluntary work in the community had caught his eye, about a bureau responsible for arranging work with the elderly, disabled, children and animals. We went straight to the website and found a possible outlet for our talents. It was a "big brother, big sister" project, designed to pair off adults with vulnerable children. We sent off for information and two days later received the application forms. References would be taken up and then we could serve both our community and our adoption interests. A woman called Ali came out to assess us and fill out the Criminal Records Bureau (CRB) forms, as we'd be working with children. She was great, so positive and so grateful that David, in particular, had applied, as they lacked male volunteers. She told us to expect a call from a child's social worker before too long. We would be able to share a variety of activities with the child and just to be there to help him or her grow. We were so excited when Ali left; we really thought maybe we were the type to adopt after all. So now at least the interim period could be filled doing something proactive, and possibly even with helping other children.

Throughout these months, we had still been seeing Ted for acupuncture and Chinese herbal treatment, trying to calm David's over-active energy channels and to maximise my fertility. Ted remained positive, and we were persuaded that we hadn't given him sufficient time. Unlike IVF, the acupuncture and herbs made me feel like a whole person, not just a set of reproductive organs. And in some peculiar way, the Chinese medicine gave me faith in the adoption route, as I started to think more broadly about the kinds of individuals we were and how we had reacted to the whole baby trial so far.

The adoption agency had told us to expect a letter of invitation to arrive in December to confirm our places on the February adoption course. The letter did not arrive, so I called them in January. Apparently they were changing their procedures and, in any case, as we wanted only a baby we would be quite far down the list. Although they were all very nice, we were made to feel rather selfish and ungrateful. They said that they'd get back to us, but in fact nobody contacted us. We waited and waited. I called them again, straining my patience and politeness. My question was long-winded and clumsy and the young woman on the end of the phone didn't even pretend to be interested. She took my details and left me on hold for almost five minutes, before picking up the receiver again with apparent reluctance:

'I've talked to my supervisor and she says we are not in a position to make those kinds of assessments right now.'

'So, there's nothing we can do?' I was struggling to sound calm.

'I understand that you must feel frustrated.'

'Yeah, right, so go and do something about it,' I thought to myself.

'In any case,' she continued, 'my boss will be writing to all the people in your position to explain the situation.' Needless to say, the letter never arrived.

Four weeks later I lay in bed one lunchtime with dreadful period pains. I'd run out of Ted's potions and I was no longer sure if they were – strictly speaking – period pains, or whether they were in fact "can't have a baby" pains. It didn't seem to matter; I felt sick, tired and spotty and retreated to the dark side of the duvet. But then a conversion of sorts happened: I sat bolt upright, slapped my face with both hands, flung my heavy legs over the edge of the bed, shook my lethargic body and shouted 'Enough!' Enough feeling sorry for myself. Why was I waiting for some hopeless or over-worked social worker to think of my needs? I jogged down the stairs, had a long glass of water, and then went onto the internet.

Half an hour later I was armed with phone numbers. I called a national line to get the number of a different local authority. I dialled the number. Apparently, they had no restrictions. The man on the end of the phone was amazingly helpful, empathetic and generous with his time and information:

'There are so many children in this country needing a home,' he said, when I mentioned the overseas option. He didn't lecture us about experience with children; just asked for a general overview of our present circumstances. We'd be contacted by a social worker soon, he said, for an initial visit. I wasn't sure how David would react when he returned home. But he smiled and just said, 'I'm glad.'

We got the forms and sent them back immediately. There were information evenings and packs to be bought. I ordered them and stopped moping.

In the meantime, I wondered again about overseas adoption and called a dedicated helpline to find out more. The woman who answered was positive, encouraging and informative. Most overseas adoptions in the UK are of children from China and Russia, she told me. I was informed that it would cost a minimum of £3,000 to £5,000 for the local authority to do the assessments, then there would be travel costs, translation services and legal fees. The total costs could be in the region of £15,000. I was worried by the fact that the money doesn't go to the families or communities the children are removed from. As a relatively rich white Westerner, what right do I have to buy a child from a poor country? I could convince myself that it would be in the child's best interests; that his or her life with me would be so much better. But could I be sure that the mother agreed to the process? Quite seriously, how could I know the child hadn't been kidnapped? A couple of days later, a report about the possible trafficking of orphaned children persuaded me that we should try to adopt a child from the UK.

At this point we were linked as volunteers with a nine-year-old boy called Jason. I was given the phone number of Jason's social worker and talked to her one evening for about half an hour. Jason was a typical but lucky case. His mum had given birth at the age of sixteen. His dad didn't want to know about the baby and the young mum couldn't cope. So Grandma and Grandpa took him in at the age of one and he'd lived with them ever since. By now, Mum had another three children by three different fathers and came over once a week, not to look after Jason but to be looked after herself, by her mum. We went to meet Jason and his grandma one evening soon afterwards. Janice, his social worker, was standing at the door.

'Hi,' she greeted us in a jolly, friendly voice. 'We're really nervous in here, aren't we?' she called back into the house. Jason was not in the least bit reticent and rushed forward to inspect these two strangers.

'How old are you? Are you married? Do you have a big car?' We were bombarded with questions, many of them mediated by Janice, who pointed out after one particularly direct question that it wasn't appropriate to ask people about their sex lives. Eventually Jason calmed down a bit and took David outside with his dog to play football. I thought David would break the kitchen window, as he struck it twice. But both of them came back in smiling. Jason obviously wanted male attention and Janice explained that his grandpa was very poorly and spent a lot of time in hospital.

'Come and see my bedroom,' shouted Jason. We went up to a brightly decorated room lined with video cassettes, DVDs and with a TV on brackets hovering over Jason's bed. Apparently he was a James Bond fan. And his collection was filled with films that I'd be too scared to watch. He explained that he goes to bed to watch TV and falls asleep with the TV on. We said nothing. We were not there to judge Jason or his grandparents. But it did make us think about the kind of parents we would be.

'When are you taking me out?' demanded Jason, suggesting a large range of possible venues to visit, each of them at a very high entry cost. We promised to take him out one week later.

During that first trip, he was grateful and polite. We

walked around the park, paid for him to go on the bouncy castle and play crazy golf, and bought him an ice cream. Just four hours. But we were completely exhausted. The following week, though, was exhausting for quite different reasons. We went to a different park with Jason, and as we walked along past a lovely family group feeding the ducks he spat on the pavement. Five minutes later he was shouting at the top of his voice, pretending to sell the watch he was wearing. And all the time his language was, well, adult. We didn't really know what to do. So we sat on a bench with him and talked to him. We explained that we didn't expect a young man to behave like this; we only took out polite boys. I sounded like a schoolteacher from Victorian times. But he was testing us, finding our limits. He'd reached them pretty quickly.

'Unfortunately, we can't take you out again unless you promise to behave better.' He calmed down and said he wouldn't do it again. And to be fair to him, he didn't. But over the next few weeks he did try a few more tricks, all neatly rebutted by our rock-solid joint opposition. It was a challenge, though, and I was starting to resent losing every Saturday morning to Jason's difficult behaviour. We agreed to move to meeting every fortnight and we slowly found the right balance.

The rollercoaster experience of our times with Jason gave us food for thought about adoption. How would we manage a child with a different background; with behavioural problems; with learning difficulties, perhaps? And yet even a short amount of time with this difficult nine-year-old was proving to be more rewarding than we'd imagined. We felt ready to go through the formal process of adoption at last. When I say "ready", I don't mean that we both woke up one morning convinced that we could or should become adoptive parents; rather, the reasons for not doing it diminished. We'd also enjoyed a succession of children-filled weekends, and were far from being glad when they went home.

It was early June and, after the previous experience with Sally, we prepared ourselves to wait for a month or so for contact from an adoption social worker. But this time was different. Within a week we'd organised to meet Sam and had a home visit set up for mid June. It was great. We just chatted with Sam about her professional experiences of caring for children in desperate situations and she asked us quite a few questions about our own failed attempts at trying for a family. She was more relaxed with us, more experienced, than our previous social worker visitor had been. She was also enthusiastic and thought we'd be good candidates. The next preparation group meeting would take place in July, she told us, but was fully booked. So she'd put us on the October one. However, as she got up to leave, Sam turned and asked:

'If I could get you on the July course, would you be able to come?' David started to stammer about a conference he was planning to attend, but I nudged him and replied, 'Of course'.

David spent the next three days trying to rearrange his presentation and promising other favours in return, as well as making up a lie about a minor hospital appointment. I know he felt it was a lot of hassle for nothing, but he was doing it for me. A few days later, though, it paid off, when Sam emailed to say there'd been a cancellation and we could join the July preparation course. The course itself was designed to give you more information about adoption and make you think through the reality and differences involved in adopting a child. For this particular agency, at least, it was also a requirement before you could apply. We were making some progress, however small.

Around this time our beloved cat died. Perhaps it was all those latent nurturing hormones, but I convinced David that we should consider getting a dog. We could keep an eye on a dog and it couldn't easily roam off like cats do.

'I'll train it and feed it and walk it,' I promised feebly.

'You sound like a little girl.'

Wasting no time, the following day I dragged David off to visit the dogs' home. And one week later we came home with a beautiful puppy we named Max. In the meantime, David had fenced in the garden and I'd attended a compulsory pet pre-adoption class. A pet was giving us a new kind of practice for a different kind of parenting experience, and adoption seemed to be the buzzword of the hour.

Finding a puppy-sitter for Max was part of the general state of excitement before our adoption preparation course. With two full-time jobs to hold down and a house to run, juggling animals and – hopefully – children would have to become part of our daily existence. David had been, and no doubt still was, very worried about the responsibility involved in owning a dog. This amused me, as the level of responsibility around child-rearing would be a million times more onerous. David's parents had agreed to dog-sit, but that didn't solve other problems: what to wear, how to arrange my hair, should David wear a jacket; would we talk too much, or too little; would we like the other members of the group? The course took place over four days and there were three social workers, two experienced adopters and only eleven potential applicants: five couples and one single woman. We were given a chance for brief introductions and handed a voluminous adoption pack of information and tasks, which would provide useful reminders after the course. There would, we were assured, be no role play, no bean bags, and no social work jargon.

I was relieved that there were no revelations about endless IVF treatment, miscarriages and broken hearts and dreams during the sessions. Some of that would come out over friendly lunches and quiet coffee breaks. And in fact, our group members all had different stories to tell. One couple had met in their thirties and decided to spend time together before even considering having children. When they wanted them, it didn't happen. The single woman had had a pretty tough life and an ex-husband who had refused to have children. That was, in part, why they had divorced, but it was too late for her to have children by then. And now she was convinced that she could give so much love to a needy older child. One couple had a difficult story of miscarriage after miscarriage and the near loss of life. They'd been through the roughest times, but were still smiling and were convinced that adoption would work for them. Another couple had a son but were told they could have no more children, so were determined to adopt a little girl.

The first day was spent looking at what adoption actually means. The real revelation to us was the fact that even if we adopted a very young baby, he or she could bring with them a serious amount of physical and emotional baggage. The second day we had to change rooms, so asked at the reception for the Carlton Suite. In a booming voice, the woman behind the counter said: 'Oh, for adoption?' I raised my eyebrows to David and we walked on. Why should she be discreet about it? Because it's private. Adoption lives in that strange no-man's land. Our business. And yet half the world – from the police to doctors and social workers, and friends who have to be your referees – has to know about it. But we need to stay in control of the information. Ultimately it belongs to us and to our child. That day we went into some rather harrowing details of the kinds of abuse adopted children might have suffered. Not just the headline-grabbing sexual abuse and physical violence, but also the subtle, often long-term effects of early neglect, of lack of stimulation and attention, which may manifest themselves fully only when a child goes through the school gates years later.

When we returned the following week, we learnt about child development and attachment patterns. We needed to remember that these children simply behave like, well, children. But sometimes adopted children have particular problems that require special attention: tantrums among older children and serious attachment difficulties for children who have been in and out of different homes for years.

The final session began with a look at the everyday challenges for adopters and moved on to look at what to do about telling your child the story of his or her life. When and how can we tell them they've been physically abused as babies? When should we inform them that they have a "tummy mummy" as well as their "forever mummy"? And how on earth would you even start to explain some of the horrific histories of daddy killing mummy, or child rape? Children's Services wanted us to be aware of all the possible scenarios; a particular child may be affected by many, a few, or none of them.

As we left, we were told that this was just the beginning and we had now to make the big decision about whether to continue on this journey. We'd learnt about what could happen when adopting a vulnerable child. But we'd also listened to real adopters and seen them glow with pride at the progress of their children: real children, their children, in thriving families. And we heard about all the daily challenges they bring: slippers flushed down toilets; problems with school work and slow development; tantrums and the refusal to eat the food they have in front of them. As my friend and mother of two boys pointed out, this sounds like being a parent.

The day we finished the course we took the puppy for a walk and then cooked ourselves a special meal, so that we could sit outside and talk over the whole process. We'd had a mini-interview that afternoon, just to review our impressions and ask any last-minute questions. We'd had none. The course had been a very positive experience and we were ready to go. We'd filled in the application by Sunday night, walked to the post-box together and, together, put the envelope into the box. Fingers crossed. For what, we didn't know. But we felt strangely elated. Within two weeks, we received a letter informing us that our application had been accepted and that we would be allocated a link worker shortly. And sure enough, our link worker, Anna, entered our lives six weeks after the preparation course, to become our closest confidante for the months ahead.

5

What about the dog?

Anna arrived at eight one dark, autumnal night. She was half an hour late, having got lost on the country roads in the dark, sat politely on the edge of our armchair and looked a bit uncomfortable. She sorted through her paperwork for a few minutes and then looked at us both.

'I suppose you want to know what I'm here for.'

And that was the start of it. During that first two-hour encounter we chit-chatted our way to getting to know each other. David and I sat hand-in-hand on the sofa; Anna gradually sank down into the armchair, as she relaxed a little. I couldn't make the puppy sit in the kitchen all that time, so had him asleep at my feet. Anna was impressed: we'd passed the initial "Is the dog safe?" test. We spent twenty minutes just looking at our diaries and trying to work out how often and how quickly we could get the six-or-so meetings out of the way. We also talked very generally about our work situations, but everything would have to be examined in minute detail in subsequent weeks. This woman would help to determine whether or not we could have a child; she would have to ask us very personal questions and would have to discuss matters we hadn't even disclosed to our families or close friends. I was very worried that I wouldn't like her. She was quite matter-of-fact and sometimes seemed to look through us. Was she bored? Did she understand our answers? And then she said something that sealed what was to become our positive opinion of her. Anna declared that she didn't hold with prevailing wisdoms; that of course we couldn't get anything like "relevant" experience by spending one evening a week with other people's children. We wouldn't have to sign up for scouts after all. Of course, we should baby-sit for our niece when possible, and our time with Jason would be highlighted, but we needn't create artificial activities in our life; activities, moreover, that would have to end on the day an adopted child arrived to take over our world. After that first evening we felt confident that Anna would help us on our way.

Within three weeks we had three lengthy meetings with her. We went through the agency's assessment form, paragraph by paragraph. Designed to capture a picture of us as prospective parents, it would be used to match us with a particular child. We covered family histories, described our own childhoods, and agreed that love, stability and opportunities were the three words we chose to take from our own backgrounds to use as parents. We weren't finding this a difficult process. Some prospective adopters have unsupportive families, difficult relationships with ex-wives, ex-husbands, and ex-lovers. And although our support network proved to be a bit tricky, as most of our friends live far away, the geographical proximity of our respective parents was crucial. We talked about ethnicity: how would we feel about having a child of dual heritage placed with us, and what, if anything, could we offer them? We discussed the problems we were not ready to take on, such as severe disabilities or children with a short life expectancy. We talked about the house and Anna saw where a child would sleep. And then we looked at behavioural issues. What would we be worst or best at? What about discipline? What would be challenging?

We got to the part in the assessment form where it mentions food and our approach to it. We could have said anything, and Anna was probably looking for phrases like "balanced diet" and "family meals", which we uttered in due course. But as vegetarians for over twenty years it was an important issue for us, and we decided to be explicit about our plans to bring up our child as a vegetarian too. Anna looked slightly uncomfortable. What about the full range of food groups? Vitamins? Societal acceptance? We'd given all this much thought and responded readily. But then she queried how a child would cope with the transition to vegetarian food. We would want our baby to feel as little disruption as possible, so I assured her that I would happily cook meat look-alikes if he or she had been eating meat in the foster home. Anna seemed to throw up obstacle after obstacle. Maybe she was testing us? Maybe she wanted to see how deeply rooted this "principle" was? She left a bit early that evening and we grumbled about her for a few days afterwards.

We did realise that the transition period can be very hard: children may have been moved a number of times already before they arrive at the adoptive home – what they need is stability. On the preparation course we met a couple of adopters who took on a five-year-old girl and, as if to compensate for a life she hadn't enjoyed up to that point, almost immediately went on holiday to Wales with her. They laughed over the total and utter disaster, but said it had been very traumatic at the time. This child didn't need holidays, didn't need to be overwhelmed by endless visitors coming to meet the new arrival. She just needed tranquility and time to trust her new mum and dad when they said that she wouldn't be moved again. After all, for her car journeys meant upheaval, not just a trip to the supermarket. So we were aware of the implications, but decided that the veggie thing was just too important for us to let go.

Things didn't go great with Anna for a while after that.

Her visits suddenly tailed off and we wondered whether her commitment to us was dwindling. We had been under the impression that Anna wanted to complete her assessment of us within three months. But she still hadn't contacted our referees. Twice she called to say that her overflowing case-load prevented her from coming out to us; and then as it grew foggy and icy she wouldn't brave the roads in the dark to come and see us at all. We were irritated. After all, we weren't applying for a car park permit.

The prospect of ever being linked with a child seemed to be growing more remote. And nagging doubts about whether it was what we really wanted were slowly starting to take root. In addition, our lives were getting busy with other projects: I was going away on a course for three weeks and we were planning a small extension to our house. We hadn't mentioned either to Anna. Even when I'd accompanied her round the house to show her where the baby would sleep and where we would be, I knew full well that those bedrooms wouldn't exist for much longer. We thought it would be easier not to mention it, and after the vegetarian nightmare we chose not to introduce any more unnecessarily complicated information. We were both happy for our meetings to be professional, rather than personal, encounters. That didn't mean we wouldn't discuss personal issues, but we were not telling her about them other than for the purpose of filling in forms.

But then, as suddenly as it had ground to a halt, the process was back on track. We later learned that council targets had to be met and we sensed that we were being pushed through to make up the quota. Having grown used to seeing nothing happen, we were actually given a date for our application to be heard by the adoption panel. Anna turned up a couple more times, asked us more questions, skated over some, and probed more deeply on others. We returned to Max the dog, who lay quietly asleep against my left leg, as Anna asked again whether he would present a danger to a child. And what if the child has asthma?

Obviously, we couldn't have a seriously asthmatic child with animals in the house. Other issues were not addressed and Anna never did ask us about our absolutely zero experience of looking after small children, so that when she left for the last time before panel she wasn't aware that we'd never even changed a nappy. I suppose those were questions for us to confront by ourselves.

Anna had interviewed a few friends and my parents. Our good friends and referees, Neil and Jane, told us that she seemed particularly worried about how we'd cope after panel, during the long wait for a placement. We were dismissive about that concern; we'd grown used to waiting and then waiting some more. We had also built a huge mental fortress around ourselves after the devastation of the failed IVF treatment.

We half-expected panel to be postponed, and knew that getting through it would really only be the end of part one. The real waiting, the real unknown, would start at that point. And with these thoughts floating between us we continued with our daily routines for the intervening weeks. In the final fortnight before the panel date, Anna punctuated almost every one of our days with calls to check numerous issues: had I got a photocopy of our marriage certificate yet? What about that query from the doctor? Had we arranged for the pond to be covered? Well, no. Some things were not going to be contemplated until after panel. She called back with possible questions we might be asked, mostly regarding our slightly vague account of our time abroad and our social network.

The night before panel we set the alarm for seven in the morning. We would need to walk the dog and leave by 8.30, to be there in plenty of time for the 9.30 meeting. We went to sleep relaxed and unworried about the following day. Rather too unworried, in fact, as we slept through the alarm and were finally woken by the dog barking at eight. There followed a very rushed breakfast on foot; David ran poor Max round the block before locking him into the kitchen; I failed to find a pair of tights without ladders. I changed into my longest skirt and vowed not to cross my legs. I'd cut David's hair for him the day before, but the new cutting machine had been sharper than I'd expected. So we spent five minutes with a pot of Vaseline, trying to cover up the bald patch I'd made on the right side of his head. I threw my hairbrush and a hair tie in my bag, along with David's tie, and we jumped into the car. As he drove along, I did my hair before awkwardly tying David's tie. He had to re-do it before we got out of the car. But before that we got completely lost. The damp patches under David's arms were starting to spread and I was trying not to panic as I read the incomprehensible map in my hand. We ended up in the car park of a cinema and were about to give up. It was 9.25am. We asked a passer-by who simply pointed slightly towards the left.

'Just there, the green building. Can you see it? You have to go back down this little road and take the first left.'

Seven minutes later we were sitting in the adoption panel waiting room. We were the only ones there; the remaining four seats were empty. A grinning Catherine Zeta-Jones looked up from the coffee table and a gallery of social services personnel looked on from the wall. After about five minutes the Chair of the panel came in. He explained who he was and the independent capacity in which he was there. He then told us that the room we would enter was full of people; that they would introduce themselves; and that we should sit next to our link worker. We were also told that our report was thorough and that there were few queries, but that they would ask us about our experience with Jason and about our neighbourhood support network.

We walked in, with our coats on our arms. David looked handsome and relaxed and I felt good to be next to him. We sat down calmly and smiled at the crowded table. We were in a square formation, with the other three sides of the table occupied by fifteen strangers. I can't remember who they all were, but there were several "independent" members, a medical adviser, a trainee social worker, an educational psychologist and others. The Chair began by asking us about our impressions of the whole process. We responded quite positively, noting that the preparation groups had been especially important. One of the independent members then asked us about Jason, and was particularly interested in the challenges he presented for us, and what we would do about him if we had a baby placed with us. That was easy. We had spent a long time thinking about him and had come to the conclusion that he was now part of our lives, not a child to be cast off at anyone's convenience. David made his audience laugh with a couple of tales of how we'd tried to stop Jason from screaming in public. One of the educational officers then asked us about how we intended to use our neighbourhood support network. We talked about our village life for a few minutes and stressed the role my parents would have. That again seemed to satisfy. The medical adviser asked us one question about our vegetarian diet and seemed satisfied with our reply about nutrition and exercise. And then it was all over.

Anna accompanied us back to the waiting room and disappeared again. She returned after only two or three minutes, to say that there were no problems: the panel would recommend our application. I suppose we should have been elated, should have been jumping for joy. But we quietly said, 'Thank you': I hugged Anna and thanked her for all her work. David did the same and two minutes later we were in the car park again. It was only 10am. So that's it, I thought. That's how approval feels. Empty. Nothing. Numb.

'Now we just have to wait for the phone call.'

And who knew how long that would be.

We went home and had a celebratory cappuccino before David went out for the rest of the day and evening. I made a few calls to family and friends. We started to think that maybe there really was something to celebrate, but we were not about to sit by the phone waiting for Anna to call. Instead, we had a small party the following Saturday and invited our six closest friends for dinner. As I served out the main course, David came in with a bottle of bubbly.

'We have some good news,' he announced smilingly and looked cheekily over at me. I smiled back, and it sank in only then that we had really been given the permission to have our own child.

'We've been approved as adopters,' he said. There was a brief silence as our friends let this sink in. Then they grinned, clapped and hugged us warmly.

'Wow, that's fantastic news!'

At times like that you really find out who your friends are. They asked us a pile of questions about the process: what does approval actually mean, do we have to do anything else, and when will the baby arrive? That was the million-dollar question.

That weekend we also found ourselves shopping in town. We needed a new toaster. We came home with three bath books for baby, a bright blue and white cot blanket and a cream towel with a hood. This, we thought, might be the start of a slippery slope, and we were right. As soon as we got home we started ripping bits of red wallpaper from the front room wall. This would become baby's room. My mum and dad were soon piling in, bringing with them a lapful of baby magazines. This baby is already part of the designer generation and he/she doesn't even exist yet. Or does she? I left David and my parents with a long list of refurbishments and headed off on my three-week course. David would also contact the builders and try and get a date for some of the internal house demolition before I got back. My trip was rewarding and consuming, but I missed David more than I could have imagined. I wondered if our mutual focus on an unreal baby had become more significant than our own relationship, and determined to pay him more attention on my return.

Almost three months to the day after getting through panel, I had an email from Anna. She wanted to check on a couple of things related to our overseas police check, for her files. There was no 'Sorry for not getting in touch earlier'. No 'I wanted to come round before now to explain everything to you'. Only this perfunctory note at the end of which she made mention of our being sent to the "consortium". I checked with David. Neither of us had ever heard of this before. Now we were joining a consortium. Was that good? A consortium of what? Of "too old to be parents of little ones"? Of "no more little white babies left"? The email ended with a promise to be in touch again "soon". Funnily enough, she had said that after the panel. So perhaps we would wait for another three months to discover what referral to the consortium would bring. (It turned out, as I discovered from the internet, that the consortium was a regional group of agencies sharing information.) It was more frustrating to hear snippets than nothing at all. Were we not even registered as being available adopters yet?

6

Enter Amber

This is the part where I should write about the miracle ending. About the mysteries of Chinese acupuncture and herbalism and that final moment of healing when all our tensions were released and our ability to conceive restored. Or about the wonders of modern medicine and the IVF process. This is the part where I should describe the day I never believed would come when I finally got the thin blue line to tell me I was going to become a mother at last. It's also the part where I tell you how David cried at the sight of his son. That really is the ending for some people. But not for us. The pregnancy has not happened and whether or not it ever will remains to be written. But we've learnt a lot about each other, about our friends, and about the wealth of life surrounding us. And most incredibly, we did get a miracle ending after all. Her name is Amber and she came to live with us in early 2007. But I'm racing ahead in our still unfinished story.

Eight months after our approval, we had received only two emails from our social worker. We actually wondered whether our file was lodged down the back of someone's untidy cabinet, forgotten forever. I had of course emailed a few times, and even left a few phone messages for Anna.

But we were not a priority. Children's Services had met their targets by getting us to panel with some haste. For the rest, they couldn't conjure up a child where one did not exist. And we were approved for a little white baby, like so many others waiting. What we didn't know then was that Anna was protecting us from disappointment. She didn't want to tell us about every possible match; only if we really might be serious candidates. She'd seen it all before and knew, better than we did, how we would react to the details of any young baby put in front of us. But for us, it was hard not to feel down. More babies were being born around us; we had stopped nipping into Mothercare; and I had stopped going down the baby aisle in the supermarket. David threw himself back into work. This was his coping strategy. Mine, in contrast, was the complete redesigning and redecoration of our house.

Dashing home from work, I'd talk to the builders who now inhabited our life, discuss fine details about window frames, lighting, and floor types. There was dust everywhere and I laughed inwardly at the thought of Anna turning up unexpectedly to view this less than comfortable and much less than safe environment for a new baby. As she didn't contact us, we didn't have to mention that our house was totally uninhabitable for animal, adult or child. The builders lived in our hair for six weeks and re-crafted our little house. It looked great, with its gleaming new windows and expanded living space. Now all we had to do was to have a new bathroom and kitchen fitted, paint and decorate everything and buy new bits of furniture. We were surviving on salads and our steamer. We didn't have any money left to go on holiday, so we bought a cheap tent and took the dog to Wales for a long weekend instead. After a soggy start to the summer, July came along with a heat wave and we had a fantastic time swimming in the sea and walking along the cliffs. We were coping, and happy.

When my young colleague and his wife announced their pregnancy, I paused, but was OK with that. The owner of our local Italian restaurant smiled pregnantly. That was fine, too. Our now ex-sister-in-law declared that she was expecting another child. No problem. But then, as I languished in bed one morning with sickening period pain, I read an article about endometriosis and decided that it described my problem. Why hadn't anyone seen it? I rushed to the internet to research private clinics. They would discover my condition, treat it and enable me to have my own baby after all. Eventually I found out that there was a gynaecology clinic near my work. I booked an appointment, and David asked if I wanted company.

'No, I'll be fine. I'm really happy about this.'

'I know. That's what I'm worried about.' He looked out from behind his newspaper. 'They may not find anything. Please don't get your hopes up.'

'I know, I know. But I just need to try this.'

For this appointment, I arrived at a new, expensive-looking glass building. Within five minutes I was face-to-face with a friendly consultant, telling him my medical and emotional history. He examined my stomach and abdomen very briefly and told me that there was really nothing wrong. How could he know that on so little evidence? And what about my pain? He did offer to transfer me to the NHS list and said he'd do a scan 'for my peace of mind'. It's not that he wasn't pleasant or kind. But I came out feeling that he thought I was a fraud. Or that, at the very least, people have much worse things to deal with and they just get on with them. David had been right, of course. As usual, I'd hoped for far too much. And the IVF examinations would certainly have picked up anything serious, wouldn't they? I drove home not really knowing what to do next. Was I really serious about adoption if I couldn't shake off this nagging hope of having my own baby?

After four years of trying for a baby, failing at IVF, hearing about the success stories of every other couple in the universe, giving up on alternative treatments and having no faith in our chances of adoption, I had nowhere to turn. And I was totally, utterly and horribly sick of keeping a permanent smile on my face at everyone else's good news. So when David told me that he knew I'd got my hopes up too much about the doctor's appointment, I went completely mad. Why couldn't we have a child? Why didn't the doctors know what to do? How come acupuncture had failed us? I collapsed in a sorry heap on the cold hall floor, where I sobbed until I could cry no more. The shaking subsided only a couple of hours later and would return intermittently during the few days that followed. David didn't know what to do, other than to hold me tight and to say nothing, or to keep out of the way. When he eventually told my mum, she was convinced that I was having some sort of breakdown and thought I should go to the doctor. Instead, David drove me over to Ted's at the end of that week. And after listening quietly to me and handing me his entire box of Kleenex, Ted administered the most soothing acupuncture I'd ever been given, and all my shaking stopped. I can't even begin to describe the sense of calm that returned to me that day. Ted also gave me an armful of potions to take away my physical pains and I resolved to put my trust back into his work. David was relieved to see his relatively normal wife come home that night, so we celebrated by watching a movie. And that was just hours before everything changed.

I was putting out the washing in the back garden the following afternoon, when the phone rang. I'd put some new photos on the sideboard in the kitchen and absentmindedly stared at them as I picked up the phone. There was a photo of David being smothered in kisses by our niece on the lawn; my mum and dad smiling awkwardly; my brother running up the garden with his dog and ours racing alongside him; and two friends holding up half-full champagne glasses on their wedding day. I'd expected David on the phone. He would almost have arrived at the train station by now and would need a lift home.

'Hello, Laurel. It's Anna. I may have some interesting news for you.'

I sensed a slightly hesitant tone in her voice, but had become inured to any communication from Children's Services and thought nothing of it. Anna continued:

'Would you like me to give you some preliminary details?'

I grabbed a leaky pen from the telephone pot and starting scribbling all over that morning's newspaper. I've kept the page. 'There's a baby girl. She's with one of our consortium partners.'

A girl – I'd always, secretly, hoped for a girl.

'She is ten months old.' It was like a birth announcement, *our* birth announcement.

'I know that you will have lots of questions, so I can give you some information now, but think it's best if I come over and talk about her in detail. I can come and see you both tomorrow, either in the morning or after 7pm.' She briefly paused; I couldn't speak.

'Anyway, she was placed in foster care immediately after birth. She was a healthy seven pounds two ounces, and seems fine generally. Obviously, there can be no full long-term medical assessment at this stage. Her mother is twenty-nine, and is in a long-term, but rocky relationship with the baby's father. We have a lot of background details about both birth parents.' She went on:

'The mother isn't a known drug user, but we are not yet sure about problems related to alcohol. As you know, the baby is too young for the doctors to be able to give any kind of definitive long-term prognosis.'

'Have you seen her?' I interrupted, still stunned by the conversation I was having.

'No, but her social worker tells me she's alert and a healthy weight.'

'What's her name?'

'Her mum named her Joley.' Not my favourite name, but I didn't care. Anyway, I thought, we can give her an alternative middle name and call her by that. I had wandered off into daydreaming mode and was way ahead of myself.

'I know you'll want to tell David, so shall we arrange our meeting?'

'Wait.' I'd collected myself momentarily: 'Are we in competition with other couples for her? I mean, I don't want to get my hopes up.'

'No, you're not in competition. The local agency is considering only you two at present. The child's social worker has seen your file and is very happy with it. Obviously, you need to make a fairly quick decision, but you should talk it over.'

'Yes, could you come over tomorrow morning, as soon as possible?'

'I can get there by ten.'

'Fine. I just have one more question right now. Is there a placement order?' I knew that without it any placement could be delayed for months and months. And could still be contested by family members.

'That is already in place. To be honest, they'd be ready to move quite quickly on this one if you want to go ahead.'

After she'd hung up, I thought of lots of things to ask. Did she have long fingers? Does she have grandparents? What state is the mother in? Is the father still around? Is he still with her mum? What colour are her eyes? I called David but his phone wasn't on. It never was. I tried to remember what he'd told me about his day's plans. Where could he be? Should I get in the car and go and wait for him at the station? I couldn't tell anyone else until he knew. I kept phoning and phoning his mobile, growing more and more impatient. I couldn't stand still. So I got in the car and drove for thirty minutes to the station. By the time I got there, he'd left me a message on my phone to say he'd be arriving soon. I only had to wait for fifteen minutes, but that was the longest quarter of an hour of my entire life. As his train pulled up to the platform, I scoured each carriage for his face but couldn't see him. Finally he alighted, and I almost knocked him over as I landed on him, arms thrown round him and babbling. Other passengers must have thought we hadn't seen each other for years. It looked like a very tearful reunion.

'What on earth is the matter?' He looked worried for a moment, but saw me grinning.

'They've got a possible match for us.' He just stared at me for a few seconds. And then he unleashed a torrent of excited questions I just couldn't answer. I'd been too mute on the phone.

When we got home we just danced around the hall and kitchen and talked in a ridiculously excited way for about five hours. The dog thought we had gone utterly mad. I'd pounce on David and say, 'Have your seen your daughter's shoes anywhere?' He left me a note on the kitchen table saying, 'Need some new clothes for our daughter.' We ate pizza, drank wine and held hands. We didn't call our parents or friends, we just wanted to savour the moment. At three o'clock in the morning we fell asleep on the sofa with the dog at our feet. When we woke up at seven we were cold and had stiff necks but didn't care. I crawled to our makeshift kitchen and made coffee. The builders arrived an hour later for an early start and joined us. We weren't exactly sure how to tell Anna about our building site, but there was no hiding it from her now. We waited for ten o'clock to drag its way to us. Anna was almost forty minutes late, and we didn't even try to act in a mature way when she arrived. We just pounced on her like excited teenagers. She laughed as she said:

'Don't you think we should sit down first?' But then she took in our house and had a brief moment of horror. Walls? Floors? Kitchen? We explained that the work was almost finished and that we could be ready very quickly. Just a matter of paint here and there. We bombarded Anna with so many questions about Joley that she didn't have any more time to ponder our strange living quarters. We found out about Joley's mum. She had had a number of health problems and couldn't look after herself, let alone a child. This was her fifth child; they were all in care. The father came in and out of her life. They seemed to need each other and to feed off one another, but there was no way they could take care of a vulnerable baby. I went to make a cup of tea for Anna, and when I returned she was talking to David about trying to explain the situation to Joley's mum.

'She knows that the baby is up for adoption and has only seen her once. She doesn't want to meet the adopters, which is unfortunate as Joley will ask you about her birth mother when she's older. But she's given us some copies of photos from when she was a child, so Joley can keep those with her'.

I'd been ambivalent about the prospect of meeting the birth parents anyway. For many people it is a positive experience, though it is invariably an emotional and difficult encounter. I wanted to know about contact with the extended family, but Anna explained to us that there wouldn't be any. Anna stayed for two-and-a-half hours and as we waved her off we were ecstatic; we were on top of the world, excited, nervous, knotted-up bundles of energy. As we walked around the garden, my mind was filled with images of a child playing with the dog, picking daisies and swinging on a pretty, as yet non-existent, swing. David went into the house for a couple of minutes and returned with my cardigan.

'Here, put this on. We're going out.'

'Where?'

'You'll find out.' He had never been secretive, and was hopeless at planning surprises. But I'd underestimated him. After driving through small village lanes for about thirty minutes, he finally pulled the car into a farmyard driveway and we came to a halt. A short, rotund man came out of the front door and waved to David:

'It's round the back.' I got out and followed the man and David, curious. And then, in front of me in a messy backyard, was the most beautiful, hand-carved rocking horse I had ever seen. It was in plain, golden pine, with a long sweeping white tail and white mane. David turned to see my face and grinned:

'Do you like it?' I loved it. 'Of course, we don't have anywhere to put it right now.'

I was in tears again by then. The day was too perfect. We had nowhere to put it. Our baby girl would be way off using it. But we didn't care. We were doing this because we loved our daughter.

Anna had left us some documents. Nothing stood out on the forms we were given. No dreadful revelations. We called Anna to confirm that we were definitely interested.

I'll never know how we made it through the next few weeks. We'd expected, naively, that we'd have our baby within a couple of months. But how wrong we were. First came the social workers from the new agency. Anna was there to support us, and the two women who came to our half-demolished house were friendly and encouraging. They wanted us to ask as many questions as possible and had not come to interrogate or test us. They filled us in on all the details about the birth parents, and told us about an older sister, Katie, who had already been adopted. We studied medical reports and one of them even offered to show us a photo.

'You don't have to look at it if you're not ready.'

We hadn't thought of photos and almost tore it from her. We held our breath. David's hand tightened around my waist. She was perfect, gorgeous. Spiky brown hair framed a fragile face and deep, dark eyes. Her almost black eyebrows and deep red lips gave her a Mediterranean hue. We couldn't speak for a few moments. Could we really be this happy? Even the sound of builders' boots in the hallway didn't faze our visitors and the tour of the half-finished house just made them laugh. As they were about to draw our first encounter to a close, one of them dropped a bombshell.

'The birth mother is eight-and-a-half months pregnant. We don't know if it's a boy or girl, but we will keep you informed about any decisions to put the baby up for adoption.'

We were speechless. Taking on board the idea of one baby was enough excitement for us for one year. They couldn't say anything else at that point, so we were left with promises of updates as they came along. A few days later we received more photographs of our lovely, brown-haired beauty. With exquisite brown, doleful eyes. Like a rabbit. My little rabbit. We were both desperate to cuddle her right then and there. We put a photo in a frame on a side table in the living room, and kept finding reasons to go and look at it.

In the meantime, we'd been given the foster carer's phone number and I spoke to her for over an hour the following evening. She said that Joley was a very easy child to care for. She obviously wasn't thrilled about our vegetarian decision, and twice mentioned how much Joley loved chicken. I didn't pursue that strand of the conversation.

One week later, Anna confirmed that we had been put forward as the potential adopters for this little girl. That evening, we drove straight over to my parents' house to tell them the good news. They didn't know anything about our recent meetings, as we just couldn't bear to tempt fate. When we arrived, we didn't even pretend to be nonchalant; my mum saw immediately that we had some news to tell them.

'You may be grandparents sooner than you think. To a little girl.'

My mum barely listened to the details; she couldn't really take it all in. After all this time, she would have a grandchild to cuddle and a funny photo to brandish. That was enough. When she'd calmed down, they both asked us lots of questions and we told them as much as we knew. But we didn't want them to tell other people; nothing was really finalised yet. We had gut feelings that this was right, and would happen; but we were afraid to admit it to anyone else. It was all too close to becoming real.

After that, the adoption panel to approve the match couldn't be convened for five weeks, and even then it was postponed for a further three. We tried to spend the time getting the house ready and, to be honest, we still had loads of work to do. Every night would see us tiling, painting, scrubbing, grouting, wallpapering, filling, sanding and trying to be arty. Some ideas worked; others had to be painted over or carefully repaired. David helped out whenever he could, especially on the wallpapering, which I could never seem to get right. We avoided baby motifs, though, and the room we planned as the nursery was painted in plain cream and white. I was too superstitious to add Pooh Bear and his friends just at that moment. Our nice builders finally said their goodbyes and banked our weighty cheque; my parents were exhausted from painting our entire downstairs; and we were in need of a holiday we were not about to take. We rushed to complete the fencing on the pond, quickly bought a cooker, childproofed cupboards and generally tried to finish the rest of the house.

We thought and thought about our daughter's name, and decided that we just couldn't call her Joley. Although we were happy to keep it as a middle name, it was not a name we would have chosen for her. Poring over the photographs we now had on our mantelpiece, we named her Amber. Anna understood our reasons, but said that we should tread carefully. She agreed to tell the child's social workers, so that they could eventually explain it to her birth parents. When they did, the birth father was very unhappy about it, but at least we'd been honest with them and this was no longer a decision he had control over. Had Children's Services or anyone else stopped us from the name change at that point, we could have changed her name after the legal hearing. At the age of one, she was not attached to her name and we had no concerns about affecting her identity in a negative way.

The birth mother had another girl, Freya. The baby had

already left hospital and been taken to join Joley in the foster home where, by all accounts, she was doing very well. Our focus was on Joley, so we tried very hard not to think too much about her sister. After all those weeks, Anna attended our matching panel and reported back that it was perfunctory and quick, although there had been one or two concerns about the proposed name change. It was agreed that, especially given the panel's own delay, introductions should begin as soon as possible. I called my parents and they rushed over with champagne. David's parents, on holiday in Spain, cheered down a crackly line and promised to drink a jar of sangria to toast our soon-to-be new family member.

Anna didn't let us down, and the following morning before ten o'clock called to tell us that we'd start introductions only two weeks from then. Only two weeks. Fourteen days. Fourteen nights of sleep before we met our child. We agreed, following Anna's advice, that we would have one week of introductions. For older children, it can be much longer. We were told that Joley was affectionate with, and attached to, her foster carers, Sue and Jim, so we would have to review the process after one week to see if she needed more time to make the transition. Such attachment was a good sign of a healthy baby, but we were petrified that she would never take to us. We bought a gorgeous little green teddy bear to take with us on our first visit. It would live with her and eventually come home with her. Meanwhile David had to get his work in order. He could still do some work in the evenings but had decided to be a stay-at-home full-time daddy for half a year. This is one huge advantage with adoption: the father can be as involved as the mother.

The plan for introductions was very detailed. We would visit for just two hours on the first afternoon, stay from mid-morning and through lunch on the second, give Joley her lunch and take her for a walk on the third, followed by a day off. The foster family would then bring her to our town and stay in a hotel. Joley would spend Friday afternoon, all of Saturday and Sunday morning with us, and be taken back to the hotel each night. Then, if all went according to plan, we'd take her home on the following Monday. While we were waiting, Anna suggested that we got on with our life story book. We bought a pink scrapbook and riffled through our photo albums, took out several black and white photos of David from birth to five; his first day at school; playing with a cat; and covered in vanilla ice cream. I added a few of my own: hugging our enormously hairy German Shepherd; sliding into water; holding a teddy bear so huge that it eclipsed all but my stumpy little legs in the photo. Indulgent and long-missed grandparents took their places next to our parents and brothers. I drew child-like sketches around the pictures, whilst David wrote a story about the little girl and boy in the pictures. This would be Joley's record of our own histories and this would become the family story she would join.

Monday morning arrived, and it was the meeting before the start of introductions. We set off on the hour's journey that would become a familiar trail. There were eight women already around the table when we arrived at the foster care centre. Each introduced herself and we chatted casually as we waited for Sue, Joley's foster carer, to arrive. She came in five minutes later and mumbled, almost immediately:

'Sorry, the plan can't go ahead.' I could feel myself go rigid.

Sue explained that her husband's mother wasn't well and they had to go and take care of her. She added that she had also decided to take Joley and Freya, her new sister, to visit their older sister, as the rather distant adoptive mother had invited them to Katie's christening. We couldn't believe it. Within seven days we were supposed to become the parents – forever – to this little girl. But at that moment no one seemed to hear our voices of concern and shock. Sue wanted to put off introductions for one week. No way. We were ready for this and had agreed to jump through all the hoops presented to us until then. Good and very experienced foster carers are hard to find and need to be treated with due deference, but during this last part of the process we found that prospective adopters sit firmly on the bottom rung of the adoption ladder. I started to cry, slightly ashamed of myself for seeming so pathetic, but so tired of having my life – and, more importantly, my child's life – in someone else's hands. Anna truly came into her own then, and became an eloquent advocate of our needs and of the child's best interests. She managed to be diplomatic but firm and for the first time we could really see her fighting on our side. She proposed a compromise solution that we readily agreed to follow. We wouldn't bring her home as soon as we'd hoped, but could spend time with her from the next day. Sue looked thunderous. She said nothing throughout the rest of the meeting and we looked forward with dread to spending the next few days at her home. We left the difficult meeting feeling shell-shocked but knowing that we would meet our daughter the following day.

We got up early the next morning and I took ages deciding what to wear. Not that Amber would have a view on it, I supposed, but when she was older I wanted to tell her everything about that day. So I wore a lovely, soft beige dress with a green scarf. I felt like a mummy. David pulled on his casual chinos and his favourite blue shirt. I knew that he was preparing himself mentally too. He held our camera at arms' length and took a close-up snap of us, as we were about to leave. We had a babbling, incoherent conversation on the way. Neither of us really cared what was said, we just wanted to arrive. These were the last minutes of our life without Amber. I squeezed David's hand as we pulled up outside the address we'd been given. Dana, Amber's social worker, was waiting in her car and waved to us. She came and gave us a hug before striding up the neat path in front of us. The house was new, airy and pristine, and I would come to wonder how anyone could look after two children and keep such an immaculate home. My stomach was churning, as much with the worry about the mood we'd find Sue in, as about seeing Amber. Dana was ready to make sure everything went smoothly, but needn't have worried. Sue smiled, welcomed us into her house and immediately ushered us through to the lounge, saying simply:

'There she is.' And there, right before our eyes, was the most perfect fourteen-month-old girl.

How can I possibly describe that moment? My brain was struggling to take it all in. We passed baby sister, asleep in a carry cot on the dining table, and headed for the noisy environment of the lounge. And there she really was. She did not look up, smile, and crawl over to me. She seemed completely uninterested in anything except the colourful game in front of her. After a few moments she turned to Sue and smiled. But then she took in the three strangers in front of her, and almost immediately started to cry. I wanted to scoop her up in my arms and give her a big cuddle, but of course I was the reason for her tears. Sue picked her up, kissed her cheek and started to talk to her gently. Amber soon calmed down and gurgled with the pleasure of being in "Mummy's" arms. How could I ever compete with that? David put his hand on my shoulder and whispered 'It's OK'. Dana stayed for about five minutes and then we just sat on the playmat and watched Amber with her toys. We didn't crowd her or try to touch her. She watched us, too, and we all slowly began to feel more comfortable. After about twenty minutes, Sue offered us a cup of tea and disappeared to the kitchen to make it. Amber looked momentarily troubled, but then carried on banging the baby drum at her feet. David took the little drumstick and started to tap out a rhythm. Amber whooped in response and banged her hands alongside the stick. In less than an hour, she was happy to hang out with us and let us play.

'Can I have a cuddle with the baby?' Sue had been so friendly that I felt that I could ask.

'Of course, I'll get her.' So I sat on the floor with a chubby sleepy baby in my arms and Amber sat beside me for a few moments watching her sister. I grinned broadly at David as I realised that this moment was the very start of our family life.

On our way home we had agreed that we would drop in at one of the centres where contact takes place in order, after all, to meet with the birth parents, who had finally agreed to see us. We had both been apprehensive about this, but wanted to be able to tell Amber that we had met them and perhaps even had our photo taken together. Anna arrived when we did and Dana reappeared about ten minutes later, looking slightly harassed.

'They're not coming.'

'Oh?'

'No, they just can't face it. I'm sorry to waste your time.'

In fact, we were both very disappointed. Having decided to go ahead with the meeting, we'd mentally planned for it. Now we would have to rely on the blurred pictures of them in Amber's scrapbook. We drove home slightly dejected, but were cheered up after spending a few minutes in Amber's bedroom.

The next day was much more relaxed. Sue was obviously a pro at introductions, in her fifteenth year of caring for newborns. She gradually, almost imperceptibly, began to disappear from the room for longer and longer periods. We just played, sang and, yes, finally, got the cuddle we'd dreamt of. She loved David and the silly faces he pulled for her. She would crawl away from him and then cheekily look back, as if asking him to chase her. And he obliged. Over and over again. One time, he caught her and swept her into his arms. She just squealed with delight. After a messy lunch, eaten in her toy car in the middle of the living room, we left feeling very positive about this whole experience.

We were early the next morning, having agreed with Sue to depart from social services' plans and to take Amber out for the whole day. By now, we had been given a very clear picture of Amber's routine, knew what she ate, when she slept, and so on. I'd asked if I could bring her lunch with me, and had enjoyed making her little sandwiches at home that morning. We drove to a large country park, not far from Sue's home. It felt amazing to turn around in the car and see Amber looking back at me, somewhat quizzically. It was a freezing cold February day, so we wrapped her up snugly and tucked her into her pushchair. After an hour's walk, we were in need of some warm tea, and pushed our daughter into the coffee shop. I wanted to shout, 'This is our little girl!'

I felt as though I'd just given birth, without the agony, blood, total exhaustion and shock, of course. I just had the exhilaration and pride. Amber sat in a highchair next to David while I went to fetch some tea. I looked back at him and saw a dad. He fitted the role perfectly. This was what we'd wanted for so long, it was almost impossible to believe that it was really happening. We gave Amber some food, with which she decorated most of the table and too much of the floor. And then we took her to the swings. She giggled and shouted 'More' every time we pushed her harder. The strongest emotions I felt during all the introductions came at that precise moment. We were doing something very simple, just like the families around us. And they didn't know our secret, because we seemed just like a perfectly ordinary family. That ordinariness was the most precious gift I could ever have asked for. Even now, whenever we go to the swings I get that sense of pure happiness that I felt on that cold and frosty day. In fact, it was so cold as the sun went down that we had to return to the car. Amber was dozing, warm as toast, but we couldn't feel our hands or feet. So we just sat in the car for forty-five minutes before we took her back. And we just looked at her. At her fine, straight hair, her long eyelashes, her rosy cheeks and ruby lips.

Back at Sue's, we tried to give her a bath. But this was too much for her. She was tired and had had enough of us. So that first bath was a brief and tearful affair, and we quickly got her ready for bed and took her downstairs for cuddles with Sue. Sue's husband, Jim, had arrived home at that point, and we felt very much like interlopers. Here we were, in his bathroom and playing with his child. But, tired as he was after a long day at work, full of cold and about to go out again to check on his mother, he was warm and welcoming and sat with us for ten minutes as he rocked Amber to sleep in his arms and let her guzzle her milk. I didn't try to quash the pang of jealousy, but I did get the chance to give Freya her goodnight cuddles as she gulped down her milk with closed, contented eyes. That evening it was very hard to leave, but we reluctantly said our goodnights and talked about Amber all the way home. She was precious and glowing and beautiful.

We were to have two days off, so that Sue and Jim could sort out their family affairs and take Amber and Freya to see their sister. The thought of them driving her such a long way filled us both with dread, but for now we were still powerless. We frittered away the two days with work and more house finishing, and couldn't wait to be back at Sue's red front door.

This time, we had lots of fun playing with Amber's toys. We told Sue about the name we'd chosen, and she said she'd use it from then on. We also talked about routines, diet, playtime, clothes and the rest of the paraphernalia of a baby's life. Some things would be changed. We only wanted to give her organic, home-made food. So we agreed that I would make some and bring it, and that Sue could add it to Amber's existing diet over the next few days. Our bedtime routine would also be slightly different. As we didn't have other children to get ready, we'd put her to bed in a quiet room on her own, and a little earlier. Sue was great. She understood that we would do things differently and respected our intentions, just as we respected what she was already doing for Amber. How things between us had changed. She gave us hints about bedtime; how Amber liked baby oil rubbing on her just before going to sleep. And she suggested that we leave some music or the radio on when we put her to bed at first, as Amber was used to having music around her. That afternoon, the last we would spend in her foster home, we left at three o'clock. As we put on our coats, Amber began to cry. We'd heard a few sobs but were not prepared for the glass-shatteringly excruciating noise she suddenly emitted. Sue was unperturbed but we were on the verge of panic.

'When she's getting tired, we do sometimes have this. She calms down quickly, though, and likes to be held and rocked. It may even be that she doesn't want you to leave.' I was sure that Sue was saying that to make us feel better, but we left with a sense of letting Amber down. We'd waited for twenty minutes and she was still crying, so Sue thought it best that we should just go.

The next day was terrible, as we were to have yet another day off. We decided to do more baby things, and added a few more decorations to Amber's room. I called Sue, just to make sure that Amber was really fine. Of course she was. And then we called a few friends. They'd supported us during these past couple of years and now could share in our joy. We also called Anna and agreed that Amber would come home with us, forever, the following Thursday. She'd spoken with Sue and with Amber's social worker and they were all happy with the way the introductions were progressing. Only six more nights of unbroken sleep, assuming that we wouldn't be too excited to get to sleep in the first place. Each of us wrote a little story about how we were feeling to put into our life story book. I called my mum for about an hour and gave her minute details of everything Amber had done. She told me about yet another celebrity who had recently adopted. I didn't care. It might be good PR for adoption, but we no longer thought about it as a process; "it" was now a child. With a beautiful new name. We took the dog for a three-hour walk and talked and talked about the years we'd just been through.

I wish I could say exactly what happened during that final week before Amber came to live with us, but it is a hazy blur in our minds. We piece it together from time to time, but we were so exhausted that I didn't keep the detailed diary I'd promised myself. I remember holding Green Teddy while Amber napped beside us, drinking in the sound of her breathing. David remembers her blue jumpsuit when we walked by the river; I remember the red ducks in the bath and how Amber laughed at being gently splashed. We both remember that dreadful feeling of having to say goodbye in those few days before she came home forever.

As planned, Sue and Jim brought Amber and Freya over to our town and booked into a hotel, before coming to drop Amber off at our house for the afternoon. She took an instant shine to Max the dog, who spent the rest of the day loving the treats but having his tail tugged. Amber's new bedroom was slowly filling up with all her toys and clothes. She spent a fun and easy day at home before we drove her back to Sue and Jim that evening. The next day followed the same pattern, with my parents coming for ten minutes, just to take a look at her. She smiled at them and giggled at my dad when he played peek-a-boo. She didn't seem to mind a bit that she was in a room full of complete strangers. When they came to pick her up on the afternoon before the big day, Sue and Jim felt as wretched as we did. I was swallowing back tears as they put Amber back in the car. But when Jim came back to say goodbye, he had tears in his eyes when he said:

'I won't get to see you tomorrow. Take good care of her.' They loved her like a daughter and had done a wonderful job of bringing her up during that crucial first year. They'd also programmed her to eat and sleep brilliantly, and to be happy and confident. We had a lot to thank them for and promised Jim that we would keep in touch.

That evening was very special. The good thing about adoption is that the night before it all happens, the woman can drink alcohol and isn't in a great deal of discomfort. David had booked a table at our favourite Italian restaurant in town. The waiter came over with a bottle of champagne and his congratulations. They knew us pretty well and David had told him it was to be a special dinner.

'Well, here we are. The waiting is over.' David paused. 'I can't believe it.'

'I can hardly eat anything. I wonder if she's sleeping. Her whole life's going to change tomorrow, too. I want her to know how crazy we are about her already.'

'I know. She will. We just have to realise that the first few weeks will be tough on all of us. She'll have to get used to a completely different environment. And she'll miss Sue.'

'Well, here goes. Here's to us.'

'Cheers. I love you.'

'I love you too.' David leaned across the table and kissed me. The diners on the next table smiled across; perhaps they thought we were planning our wedding. No, we were planning our family.

So, finally, here it was. That day we'd been dreaming of. We were getting dressed to go and pick up our daughter. We drove first to the foster care centre to dispense with all the formalities. Sue wasn't very well, so she'd sent her apologies, but told Dana that the introductions had gone 'brilliantly' and that we'd be 'wonderful' parents. We were touched. The meeting lasted only about twenty minutes. Everyone was satisfied and Dana produced some sandwiches for us to eat with her before going to fetch Amber. We'd agreed not to arrive too early, but to let her have lunch and get ready for her nap, so that she could sleep in the car. Sue's support worker had offered to go and sit with her, but she told us that Sue would rather be alone for a couple of hours to get on with everything. After all, she still had Freya to take care of. We arrived on time, waited for Dana, and then we all went to the back gate. Sue opened it, looking tired and longing to get this moment over with. Everything was packed up and David took the remaining things to the car. I had written a card to Sue and Jim and put it on top of the bread bin. Sue kissed Amber and then handed her to me. Dana lingered, checking that Sue would be OK, but soon followed us out. Sue wanted to close the door. Amber was leaning back towards Sue, so I handed her quickly to David and turned to call goodbye. As she closed the back gate, I wondered if Sue would collapse. I'd call her later, to tell her that Amber was fine, but also to check on her.

David fastened Amber into her car seat, as if he'd been doing it since the day she was born. Green teddy was fastened in next to Amber in the middle of the back seat and I slotted myself in next to him. She played with the teddy mobile in front of her for a while and didn't seem to notice that Sue was missing. David turned round and grinned.

'All in?'

'All in.'

'Shall we go home then?' And that is precisely where we went.

By the time we pulled out of Sue's avenue, Amber was already asleep, exactly as Sue knew and planned that she would be. For the rest of the long journey home, I just stared at her and kept my right hand on David's shoulder as he drove his family home. Finally, we pulled up in our drive. David lifted Amber out of the car and, whilst I gathered up as many of her things as I could carry, he took her in and put her down gently in a rocker on the wooden hall floor. She was still sleepy and had been to our house only three times, but took everything in her stride. Crawling immediately out of her chair, she wandered off down the corridor to explore. We coaxed her into the lounge and sat together on the bright red scatter cushions.

She plucked at the curtain and then giggled as we flicked through the pages of *Ten Tiny Tadpoles*. She behaved as if she were out to impress us: she ate her teatime snack happily, played cheerfully with us for the next three hours, had a big dinner, squealed with delight in the bath and then curled up to sleep in a cot-bed she'd only once napped in. We hovered over her and watched her sleeping for about forty-five minutes, and kept finding excuses to go back and check on her for the rest of the evening. The strangest thing to get used to was that she wasn't going back. Ever. We were finally a normal, everyday family. And being normal was suddenly a very special feeling.

7

A family of three

We looked every day for transition problems, but there weren't any. Amber woke up on the first morning with a smile, sat in her highchair without complaint and wolfed her Weetabix. She played with her new toys, seemed happy to be in her new bedroom, and greeted the many new strange faces with contented gurgles. She was completely unfazed by the upheaval in her life, and within a matter of a few days had become very affectionate and knew that we were Mummy and Daddy. I had to go back to work and leave David to enjoy his new life. Before we knew it, we had a family routine. I would do morning cuddles and breakfast, giving David time to get dressed. And then I'd hand her over to her beloved Daddy. They would stand at the window and wave me off, and I'd drive to work thinking about this new, strange and wonderful feeling of being a family. Everyone assumed that I must be finding it very hard to be back at work, to be away from my little girl. But if I'm totally honest, I was very happy. I had it all. A wonderful husband, gorgeous child and great job, although I tended to rush a few things towards the end of the day so that I could get home in time for her tea at 5.15. I did find that my mind wandered occasionally at work. I had a screensaver of the photo of Amber the first time we met her and found any excuses to gaze at it. When I got home I'd creep in quietly, to stand for a few minutes and watch David feeding Amber. She'd look at him and laugh, saying 'More', banging her spoon on the plate, enjoying Daddy's gourmet cuisine. David discovered a new side to himself during the months after Amber arrived, playing, cooking and loving his way into parenthood. One joy of adoption is that both parents start from the same point. One social worker did raise her eyebrows at our decision, but at that time it made sense for David to be the primary carer for a range of reasons, not least because of the flexibility of my own job and because we'd be able to manage better financially that way. However, it also meant that David had to make the greatest adjustments to our new lifestyle. He suddenly found himself alone with the responsibility of looking after this very young child on his own. He arranged their days carefully and they went out and about all over the place. They would play together with toys at home; watch a couple of DVDs; take the dog – soon Amber's very best friend – out for long walks; do some shopping and have lunch before Amber's nap; play some more and wait for Mummy to come home. He went to two baby and toddlers groups, where he was spoiled as often being the only man among the mummies. Sometimes David found the whole stay-at-home-daddy business a bit mind-numbing, especially when Amber was sniffly or grouchy. But usually, he wanted to make the most of every day of his six months off. On week nights he ploughed ahead with his work, and I even wondered if becoming a father might have made him more efficient and creative.

'Children change your life, don't they?' We were asked that question a lot, but couldn't really see what had changed, apart from the arrival of one special little girl. The secret ingredient was that we had no sleepless nights. Amber was always asleep by six, and rarely stirred before 6:20 the next morning. So we could spend every evening together, just as we always had done. We would have loved to have Amber from the day of her birth – and I would love to have been the one to give birth to her – but we did feel the benefit of having been given a perfect, and perfectly routined, child. We were not convinced that we'd have been as great as Sue and Jim during those early months. In some respects, it was so ideal that we were still hesitant to acknowledge Amber as our own, not quite believing that she was here to stay. When I took her to the baby and toddlers group a couple of times, I found myself blurting out, 'Amber's adopted,' to anyone who'd listen. Partly afraid that she wasn't yet really "ours", I think that I was also trying to avoid any possibility of being asked about the birth and early months. After about five or six weeks, I realised that I no longer mentioned it in new situations and that people could take us and our daughter as they found us.

We were only two weeks into this new set of routines when something happened to spoil our quiet life. I headed off to work as usual and called David in the morning to check that all was well at home. He sounded relaxed, said they'd been for a long walk and that Amber seemed a bit tired. When I pulled up outside the front door later that day, I noticed nothing out of the ordinary. I walked into the hall and took my time to take off my coat, and put my bag and shoes away. I smiled as I peeped round the kitchen door, but was not greeted by the usual sweet scene. There was no dinner on the table, or cooking. I thought David must still be out, perhaps with the dog. At that moment, Max appeared, wagging his tail. I wandered around the house and gradually found signs of a hurried departure. A bag grabbed and dropped in Amber's bedroom, some clothes on the floor, her curtains closed. I was just confused. I called David's mobile, but it was switched off. I was now starting to get a bit worried. The phone rang at this point and I heard my mum's voice:

'It's OK, but Amber is in hospital. She's had a febrile convulsion. David is with her right now. They're in Ward F in the Children's Wing of the hospital. You need to pack a bag for her, some pyjamas, some toys, and a sweater for David.' I couldn't seem to move very quickly to get myself out of the house. Instead, I meandered from room to room randomly filling a small blue rucksack. The doorbell rang. I opened it to the next door neighbour, Annie:

'Is she OK?' She obviously knew more about all this than I did.

'I've just got home,' was all I could say, 'I need to go to the hospital.' I drove past the dual carriageway exit and went about ten miles out of my way to get to the hospital. I was in a daze, and couldn't begin to imagine how David was feeling. Finally, I parked the car and went to an outside reception.

'What is the patient's name?'

She must have thought I was mad, I didn't know what to say. What should I call my daughter? Somehow, calling her by her birth name didn't seem right. But I stammered out the name eventually and hurried off to the ward. The nurse showed me into a whitewashed single room. David turned to look at me. He was ashen.

'I thought she was dead,' he kept repeating. Amber was in his arms, awake but not quite herself and clearly unhappy. They'd had to do some tests on her; she hadn't been to sleep and looked very pale.

'They need us to get a clean urine sample, so we have to chase her around with this.' He held up a plastic container like the ones you buy olives in. We both went to the playroom with Amber, and for the next hour we followed her around the room with our olive tub, hoping that we could catch a sample. I went out to get a couple of mugs of tea.

'Drink this. I've put sugar in it. Now, tell me everything.'

'She was fine. We'd had a nice walk. She ate lunch. She seemed very tired, but nothing to worry about. I put her in her bed and she slept for about an hour. It was when she woke up that it all began to go funny. She started screaming, and wouldn't stop. I held her, talked to her and tried to calm her down. But then suddenly she started to shake violently, and began to fit.' He paused, and shook his head in disbelief at the memory.

'I didn't know what to do. The shaking just carried on. I ripped off her clothes, and put her on the floor. But the fit wasn't stopping. I put a sheet over her and ran next door. Annie was great. She rang the ambulance for me. We both went home to wait. I just stood at the door with her. But it got worse, because the fit had stopped and I thought she was dead. She was so still, empty. Then the ambulance arrived, with an ambulance car behind it. Your parents drove up at exactly the same time, to see me standing at the front door holding the limp body of our child, covered over with a blanket. The ambulance men were great, and calmed me down as they took Amber and put her on a stretcher. They insisted that I put my shoes on, I didn't want to. But I got into the ambulance and just looked at her all the way. She started to come round, but she wasn't quite right. And since we got here, they've been doing tests, to try and find a source of infection. That's probably what caused her to overheat and fit.' David put his head between his knees. I held his shaking shoulders.

'It's OK. I'm so sorry I wasn't there.'

'I love her so much, Laurel.' There was no turning back from that moment, she was our daughter and we wanted to protect and love her forever. We looked up to see Amber weeing all over the floor, and both of us just started to laugh, and laugh some more.

'That's my girl,' said David. And he meant it.

Naturally enough, doctors and nurses kept asking whether this had happened before, and whether she was allergic to X, Y and Z. We didn't know. We were still strangers in her life. One doctor made us feel inadequate, even negligent. For a few moments we really wondered if we had done something wrong. Was her room too hot? Did we put too many clothes on her? Had we missed some key signs? But they did more tests, found a possible source of infection and a lovely consultant came to talk us through everything. He assured us that this is a very common condition in young children, that it may happen once, or several times, at random. And that it wasn't our fault. We just needed to give her a bit of medicine if she looked as though she'd overheat, and know what to do if it happened again. He gave us a leaflet and nodded to the cubicle next door.

'That six-month-old girl has come in for exactly the same reason.'

Amazingly, we managed to get back to normal very quickly, and forced ourselves not to be over-protective parents. We did make sure that she was generally cool, and never over-dressed her. We'd told Children's Services about the incident and they weren't at all bothered, except to know that she was fine now.

'You did everything you should have done.'

David and I were mildly amused that although the local authority still had some parental responsibility for Amber, they hardly rushed to the hospital when we called them. And they certainly didn't stay the night with us when it happened again. It was six months later, when Amber was twenty months old, and David had brought her to my work. I went off for a meeting for one hour, leaving David and Amber in my office. As the meeting finished I walked back down the corridor and bumped into a colleague.

'Is my cherub running wild?' He tried to smile.

'Erm, I've just called the ambulance, she's having a fit.'

I ran back towards my room and David came towards me with Amber in his arms. I took her from him and looked down at her. She was white, her eyes were open but she wasn't seeing, and her whole body was convulsing. David had put her in the pushchair where she'd fallen asleep, but suddenly heard a strange sound. He leapt to her and saw that she'd started to have a fit. We carried her downstairs together and waited outside for the ambulance. I put her on the grass, naked. People I hadn't seen for ages just kept appearing and looking awkward. It was quite a surreal scene. The ambulance took only a few minutes, but it seemed like an age. Amber stopped fitting and went into that dreadful silent mode. I could only imagine how horrible it had been for David to go through all this on his own. She then stirred and vomited horribly.

The ambulance men were great, stayed calm and explained what was happening. We pulled up at the hospital and they put her on a trolley. She looked tiny and very, very fragile. This time it wasn't quite so straightforward. We were at a different hospital, different doctors. We were put in a waiting area, but Amber's left hand started to shake, then her leg. She was going into another fit. We called the doctor and he quickly moved her to a screened-off bay. He monitored her carefully, but was starting to look worried. He went to fetch his senior colleague and she suggested that he administer anti-fitting drugs. Amber had been convulsing on and off for over an hour and they weren't happy with her state. In the end, they had to dose her with three lots of anti-fitting drugs and finally she was still. She was so beautiful, and looked like an angel in a coffin. We kept checking her breath. Because of the quantity of drugs Amber now had inside her, they took her up to the High Dependency Unit, where we stayed for the next twenty-four hours. The doctors asked us lots of questions, and this time we were confident and firm in our replies. This was our baby and we knew her. By 10:30 that night, she'd been asleep for nearly nine hours and hadn't moved. The nurses had been in and out, made us cups of sugar-loaded tea, and asked if we were OK. I was starting not to be. Would she have brain damage? Would she wake up? They tried to reassure us, but couldn't say anything definitive until she'd woken and they'd done some tests. Finally, at 11pm she woke up and screamed through the rest of the night. I've never been so happy to hear a child cry. Ten hours later, the consultant was fantastic when she came to tell us how satisfied they were with the results of the tests. She even told us not to cancel our holiday plans. We'd assumed that our trip to Italy two days later would have to be postponed. But we did go, and had a great time. The only precaution we took was to check the location of the nearest hospital to our hotel.

Those two horrible incidents sealed our bond with Amber. David had formed a very close relationship with her and it was wonderful to see them together, Daddy and his girl. I would spend as much time with her as I could but the honeymoon of motherhood ended for me after about three or four weeks. I felt guilty for thinking this way: wasn't this what I had dreamt of for years and years? Looking back, I think that things were just becoming normal. One of my friends said, before Amber arrived, that children are 'everything'. I thought about her words a lot. Children are joy, total happiness. But they are also boring and dull at times. I didn't regret our decision for one moment, but I was getting a good dose of real life. And I wasn't even the one at home all day. David said he knew what I meant, and that was why his trips to the gym some evenings were so important. And why he was glad at the thought of going back to work eventually. That feeling of slight frustration had come on quite suddenly and, without my noticing, it was replaced before long by a gentle accommodation to our new lifestyle. Somehow, some way, Amber was managing to crawl under our skin and by the time of the second convulsion we felt the most profound, almost painful love for her. Perhaps she'd grown up a bit, developed a personality. We'd all got to know one another and already had our own family history to share. When I held her sometimes, I thought my heart might fuse with hers, she had become such a precious and core part of me.

During the first few weeks and months after adopting a child, there are a number of reminders that you are adopters and not birth parents. Apart from being unsure about Amber's medical history on that first night in hospital, we also had weekly, and then bi-weekly, visits from our and Amber's social workers. They were visiting only to check that everything was all right and were simply fulfilling their statutory responsibilities, but it did feel as though we were still under the microscope. I was usually at work when they arrived, so David made them a cup of tea and explained that we really – really – had no problems. They were happy with our response to Amber's febrile convulsions, but we generally kept the tone low-key and didn't get into any details about our emotions. Anna had told us of a "buddy" scheme, to link us to an established adopter, so that we would have someone in our position to turn to if we needed advice. We weren't silly enough to say no, and knew that there might be moments to come when we'd need help. So we started to speak to Sally once a week, but it didn't last long. She'd adopted a five-year-old boy with many special needs, and had struggled from the first day with his health problems and learning problems. We couldn't relate to any of her stories and when she finally came over for a coffee, she was surprised to find that we really didn't have any issues to share with her. We did talk about life story work, and she gave us some good ideas about what to include. Another friend was matched with a perfect "buddy", someone who'd experienced more or less the same set of circumstances as she had. They talked on the phone at least once a week and my friend found her an invaluable source of practical tips and emotional support. In our case, though, we all knew before long that we wouldn't be staying in touch.

After only three weeks we had a formal review with the social workers and an Independent Reviewing Officer. He was perfectly satisfied; the meeting lasted an hour only because we padded it out with chit-chat and the Reviewing Officer spoke very slowly. And that, more or less, was it. After ten weeks, we were able to lodge the papers for Amber's formal adoption. This took much longer than we expected: we needed all sorts of details we didn't have to hand; Amber's social worker needed more time to complete her report; and the first court date was cancelled because the judge couldn't attend. Altogether, it took about nine months from the time Amber came to live with us to complete the process of legal adoption.

The day we went to court was a very special one. Amber behaved like an angel and stole the day. We had invited a number of friends and family and were amazed at how many people turned up. The judge said she'd never seen so many people at an adoption hearing. Three of our best friends came, complete with a large bunch of flowers; an auntie and godparents David hadn't seen since our wedding were there; and my mum and dad brought Mum's cousin and his wife. The room was full of smiley, chatty people and Amber was playing with the microphone, when we were asked to stand for the judge. A smart and friendly looking woman came in and immediately welcomed us all. She asked us who we all were, and Amber was soon introducing everyone by herself. The formalities lasted only a few minutes and Amber, in proud possession of a certificate and *Mr Men* book, was allowed to sit in the judge's seat and call her audience to order with the gavel.

'You've got your hands full there,' the judge nodded indulgently at Amber.

Thanking us all for coming along, the judge told us that this was the very best part of what can often be a rather depressing job. She also has to take the decision to put children in care in the first place, and so is very happy to see them find the home and family they deserve.

Our troupe journeyed in convoy back to our house, where my homemade bright green dinosaur cake and lots of balloons were waiting to accompany the champagne chilling in the fridge. This family gathering was matched by a second party for our littler friends the following Saturday, when the house was turned completely upside down by eleven children. Amber had taken our name and had become a fully fledged member of our family, so a double celebration was the least we could do. My parents were especially ecstatic, as my mum had harboured a nagging worry that if something happened to us before Amber was formally adopted, then she would also lose her granddaughter. Now, nobody could take Amber away from her new family.

We called Sue and Jim every night for the first two weeks Amber was with us, and then every couple of weeks after that. They so obviously loved Amber that we didn't want to take them away from her. After about two months we all thought that it would be fine for Sue and Jim to bring Freya over for a visit. It was a hot day, our patio doors were open wide, Amber was busy pushing her little car round the garden, and I was making some cakes when they arrived. The visit was strange for two reasons: Amber ran to the front door when the bell rang to see who the visitors were, but showed no sign at all of recognising this couple who had been her mummy and daddy for over a year. She smiled at them, and was happy after a few minutes to take them to the garden and play with them. But they were not special guests like Grandma and Grandpa. They were just more playmates. That must have been hard for Sue, after all the tears she'd shed for Amber, all those sleepless nights in her early weeks, all that love. But she was used to it, and took it with good humour; genuinely happy to see how well Amber was developing. Jim was thrilled to see Amber, kept throwing her up in the air and held her hand as they walked round and round the garden. The visit was also strange because they brought Amber's baby sister with them. She giggled and gurgled in her carry-cot and let us give her cuddles and make a fuss. But it was hard right then for us to imagine that she might ever join us. We were just getting used to the idea of being a family of three.

8

Ups and downs

There is so much pressure for adoption to be perfect, that if the slightest thing goes wrong you risk feeling that you've failed. We spent months and months trying to convince Children's Services not only that we'd be the best parents, but also that we wanted to be parents more than anything else in the world. So it was a shock for us to discover that not every moment was idyllic: I was never going to raise my voice as a mum, but I did; I'd never have imagined that I'd need to call on the help of a neighbour, but I did; and I was convinced that I would balance my professional and family life just as easily as I'd managed before, but it wasn't as easy to juggle a child and work. While being thrilled and feeling privileged to be a family, we also had to face the reality of changing nappies, and of having food sprayed all over the walls. Talking with friends who were dealing with early parenthood themselves, we soon came to see that the ups and downs of adoption were simply the ups and downs of being a family. And although on paper we knew how we would respond and exactly how we would act, we had to improvise from the moment Amber came to live with us. At the age of fourteen months, she knew what she wanted and we would have to take our cue from her.

People say that you don't realise how hard it is to be a parent until you've given birth. When you're adopting, it is hard not to compare yourself to birth parents who have about nine months to prepare mentally and physically for the new arrival. They have a socially scheduled timetable for tests and public announcements. They can then grow together with that new baby and anticipate the development of a little individual. Social workers dictate how long you have to get used to becoming adopters; there is no pregnancy announcement after the reassurance of the twelve-week scan; there's no little hint of a bump to get people talking (although, when you've been together for as long as we have, they're talking anyway). And you haven't the vaguest idea about the combination of genes your little bundle might bring with her.

Over and over again I'd wished for the experience that pregnancy would bring. But giving birth also involves fears and uncertainties, after which you are left with a fragile newborn child for whom you have one hundred per cent responsibility. There can be an enormous amount of insecurity and uncertainty before an adopted child arrives, but at one year old she is not fragile. More importantly, given a good start with her foster carers, she has also been trained to sleep through the night; has been introduced to a wide range of foods; has been transferred from a cot to a bed; has been given her MMR inoculation; and has already become a fully fledged happy, healthy and thriving child. We were not deprived of our sleep or terrified that she might stop breathing every time we left the room (at least not until the convulsions). And we knew that we could call the foster carers with any questions we had. Or the local authority. Or expert advisers. Her age also meant that she had been left from time to time with a babysitter, so that we weren't afraid to go out occasionally and to carry on doing the things that made us a couple. Friends who had recently become parents told us that one of the hardest things for them to do was to leave the child with anyone else. They couldn't believe that we went out for an evening just two weeks after Amber's arrival.

We did have to get used to changing our clean, tidy and quiet home, to accommodate a messy and noisy baby and her sacks and cupboards full of toys and clothes. The house was not ours any more and there were signs of Amber in every corner. We came very quickly to love these constant reminders of her, but it did jolt us into the reality of family living. Adopted children should come with a baggage warning. At our preparation group, we'd heard a story about two children who had arrived at their new home with just a small black bin bag between them; our child's stuff could have filled a bin lorry. Amber had had her first birthday and Christmas just before coming to us. We should have hired a van to bring her home really, and the one advantage of the protracted introductions was that we could get everything in the car bit by bit. By our first Christmas together, we were begging people not to buy presents and still the bottom half of the tree was invisible. I'd pulled a couple of existing toys out of the loft and wrapped them up as presents. There was just no point in getting anything new.

When the next-door neighbour moved, she kindly brought us all her children's things. We had presents from everyone we'd ever met. There was the moving in day; birthday; adoption day; Christmas. One colleague at work left a bag as tall as I am, full of children's clothes, and I soon realised the enormous advantage of being such an "old" parent: all of our close friends were years ahead of us and just at the point of handing their children's things on. Our loft is now full of giant cuddly toys and black bin bags labelled "0-2"; "3-5"; "over 5". I'm not planning on clothes shopping until Amber is well into her school years. Nor do we need any more toys, as we have enough to fill Hamleys: from activities for learning numbers, spelling and colours, to full-sized jigsaws and books for eleven-year-olds. Although the old shoe box by the back door is more exciting than any of those shiny things at the moment, I'm sure we'll get through many of these loft dwellers eventually.

Adoption is a funny business. Our neighbours on one side had never really taken to us and seemed to think of us as two neat professionals who didn't like children. With their four children, they clearly thought we were abnormal beings, those "professionals", or "that career woman" – all derogatory terms for someone not able to see that having a family is the be all and end all of life. From the day that Amber arrived, however, besides coming round with bags of clothes and toys, they smiled at us, and felt able to relate to us as parent to parent. They also took us along to the new local toddlers group, which made the whole experience slightly less intimidating.

After six months, and only two days after her second convulsion, we took Amber on holiday. She was entertaining and gorgeous to travel with – patted her seat on the plane, said 'Hiya' to everyone who boarded after us, and 'Bye' as they filed out when we landed. She played a bit, ate a bit and obligingly slept a bit while we were in transit. When we landed in Italy, I was paranoid that the immigration officer would question us about her passport: why are we travelling with a child who does not have our name? We had a letter from Children's Services to confirm that we had their permission to take her on holiday, but it was in English and, frankly, could have been forged by a child. I know that some local authorities discourage you from taking children out of the country before they are legally adopted. But we had spent half a year preparing for Amber's arrival and we needed a short break. As our friend was getting married in Italy, it seemed like the perfect opportunity. Amber was the centre of attention for the entire week. She ate all the new foods we introduced her to, and discovered a love of pizza I think she'll have forever. She adored the seaside, ran and ran around the piazzas and bounced and bounced on the hotel bed every morning and night. We went on trains, trams, in taxis and for long walks. She loved the variety and the colours and greeted everyone who would smile at her.

On the day of the wedding we all dressed up, and Amber looked like a doll. The whole ceremony and reception lasted from 2pm to well after midnight. Amber ran around the courtyard as we waited for the ceremony to start, played up as our friends said their vows (we took it in turns to take her outside) and threw her food around during the meal that followed. We started to worry when the speeches didn't begin until 11pm. Amber refused to go to sleep in her pushchair, and insisted repeatedly that we take her down a dark side alley where the twinkling lights on her shoes could be fully appreciated. As we collapsed into bed at 1.30am, Amber fell asleep between us and stayed there all night. She was using David's bottom as a pillow when I woke up the next morning.

The holiday had been brief but delicious and I'd forgotten any anxieties, until we got to the airport to go home. The grumpy looking official took our passports and handed them back fairly quickly. But then, as we were about to walk away, he called us back. He scrutinised our passports once again and started asking questions in faltering English. I wanted to explain to him in Italian why Amber had a different name, but he insisted on conversing in English and we weren't getting very far. For the next twenty minutes we struggled not to get frustrated as he insisted that he wasn't happy with the letter from Children's Services because it had no stamp on it. I could feel my cheeks getting hotter and hotter and hated the fact that I had to explain all this. It was a painful reminder of our current status as prospective adopters: that we still had to finalise the legalities and that we still didn't have full responsibility for our daughter. In fact, right then we felt as though we had borrowed this child for our holiday and that she didn't really belong in our family.

One negative experience couldn't dampen my

overwhelming sense of amazement that we'd become parents. I felt like a mother most of all when I was walking down the street with my baby. My baby. The public face of motherhood for me was the point at which it became real. I grinned as I lingered over a caffe latte in Starbucks. I'd joined the league of proud parents: I didn't want to shout it from the treetops, but nor did I want to be too quiet about it. I have the right, at last, to behave like a woman who has a baby. To be a typical mummy. The problem, if it was a problem, was that I certainly could never be typical, as I was reminded every time I took Amber to the baby and toddlers group. The conversations of the other women focused on birth. Many of them were pregnant with their second, third, or fourth (or fifth) child, and even those who knew me often forgot that my child was adopted. Forceps. Long, agonising labour. Just made it in time. Degree of dilation. I soon had enough information to invent the birth of my child if I had wanted to. Instead, I would remain quiet and smile, hoping that Amber would want to play with me and demand my attention. During those times, and elsewhere, I didn't really know when or where to say, or not to say, that my child is adopted.

One morning the chiropodist chatted away at a million miles an hour, my feet in her hands, and rattled on about her children. When she found out that I had a one-year-old daughter, she asked a hundred questions about Amber's early months.

'Was she a good sleeper?'

'Was she premature?'

The questioning was interminable, but I went past the point where I could tell her the truth and ended up fabricating stories about Amber's early days. The woman at the supermarket checkout almost caught me out too, and I felt myself going pink with all the lies I was telling. People ask such personal questions, but only in the same way they talk about the weather. It's just something to talk about, so I don't feel that I have to tell the truth or keep it a secret.

And for a while my response depended on where I was and the mood I was in: sometimes I'd state in a matter of fact way that she was adopted; other times I'd be vague and make little sense; and once or twice I would just lead the listener on to believe that I'd given birth to her. I gradually began to feel comfortable with the fact of being a here-and-now mother, and stopped worrying too much about the story I wanted to tell.

Later, when I returned to work after taking leave with Freya, my office secretary told me that she'd explained to students that I was on maternity leave. She felt that telling them I was on adoption leave was somehow more private, that it would perhaps lead to too many questions. She was just trying to protect me, and reacted as I had sometimes done. Because don't onlookers jump to immediate conclusions about possible infertility, and do you want people's pity or curiosity? Also, wasn't it an intrusion into the child's own personal story? But part of me resented her not having simply told the truth. We have every right to be proud of our adoption story and, after all, is it much different these days from many of the other complex family stories children bring with them to the school playground?

Everyone was amazed at how much physical resemblance there is between Amber and me. Casual observers tell me we have the same eyes and, although I don't see this myself, I am hugely flattered to hear it, as somehow it makes her belong to me more fully. I tell myself that as she develops she is likely to adopt many of my – and David's – little physical habits and movements, as children often resemble their parents in that way. But I also know, if I'm honest, that our similarity strengthens my confidence in public to be the mummy to this child, to believe that we were meant to be together.

Some people implied that Amber seemed to be developing according to average milestones and that we should feel lucky to have picked such a healthy child. This kind of remark is often not intended to cause offence, but it is quite an ugly thing to say. Children develop well or badly in different areas for all sorts of reasons. Amber may grow very tall, stay very small, be very bright or find it rather hard to learn, she may develop physical limitations or have a serious mental condition. And we didn't pick her as a future prospect, like some bet on a horse. Whatever her future, it will be as our daughter, as part of our family, and we'll take each day as it comes, just like any other parents. We do feel very lucky that we and Amber have found each other, but because she is our child and we love her, not because she is better or worse than any other child who might have joined us instead.

I had a different problem with a senior colleague. As a departmental boss, he would send emails of effusive congratulations to anyone who had a birth to celebrate. I did not get a celebratory email, nor did he congratulate me personally on our news. Instead, he told me that he was glad I wasn't entitled to paid leave, as he wouldn't have to find cover for my teaching. And although his son is the same age as Amber, he has never asked even one question about how my daughter is doing. I sense that he would find it hard to utter those words to someone who hasn't given birth. These are the kinds of people that make it hard for me to accept the term "natural" mum. "Birth" mum, or even "biological", are fine; they do not suggest that, by implication, I am an "unnatural" mum. Perhaps I'm too sensitive after all these years and maybe my sensitivity will diminish with time. But a word of congratulations in recognition of our happiness wouldn't have gone amiss.

Having Amber perfectly fulfils my desire to be a mother, but that doesn't mean I know what it feels like to carry a child to term inside me. I have spoken to a few other adopters about this and they do not seem to feel as I do. They may be in denial, or they may honestly have got everything they want. For me, the four-weekly reminder of infertility is lingering around, at least for now, so if I thought adoption would make that pain go away, I was wrong. I would not be without Amber for all the babies in the world now, but my body still tells me that it hasn't achieved what it was intended for. It's that simple: my mind and heart have everything they need, but my empty womb doesn't. I deal with it in a very practical way and just allow those feelings to flow over me in waves from time to time, before getting on with my family life. I've got far too many blessings to count to feel the way I did before, so it's a longing I can safely store away.

We look at Amber and wonder what she will become, what she will do with her life. At the age of two, she is healthy and happy and we are steering clear of any books telling us what her next developmental milestone should be. Most of the time we deny the possibility that anything could ever go wrong and we agree that all we can do is to cross any difficult bridges if and when they appear. We try not to think too much about the history of Amber's birth parents, and prefer to believe that any problems they have in their own lives come from choices they themselves have made, and have not been passed on through genes from one generation to the next.

Our niece came over with the family tree she'd been making at school the other day. I wondered what Amber's family tree would look like. Is your family tree your bloodline? Does Amber's family tree now bear our name and history? In reality, Amber has two family trees and we can't and shouldn't deny the existence of the other one, even if we don't know it all, and even if we wish we could erase it. And nurture, we hope, will get us a very long way, but at times genes may win out and that is a prospect we have to be ready to deal with if it becomes real. All of these feelings and worries can be gently packaged and stored; to dwell on them would not help us and would do no good.

One huge issue in adoption is the extended birth family. Not just the birth parents, to whom we write once a year and send a couple of photos; not just grandparents and assorted aunts and uncles, who seem to get forgotten in the process; and not just half-siblings, who go on to lead their own, separate lives; but also, and most importantly, full siblings who are adopted elsewhere. In our case, Amber came with a ready-made older sister. We'd seen photos of her and, although she bore a passing family resemblance, we couldn't really trace a family line to Amber's face. More problematically, the sister's adoptive parents didn't want to maintain face-to-face contact with us. They were keen to protect their daughter and believed that telling her about adoption at the age of three or four might be detrimental to her. So they kept her away from Amber. They had also had a fairly bad experience with Children's Services and were no longer on speaking terms with their social worker. Even more significantly, they had hoped to adopt Amber and had been led to believe that she would eventually join them. According, at least, to the story we were told, the local authority had never considered that plan, as the couple had required considerable post-placement assistance with Katie, the older sister, and social workers did not believe that they could deal with two children.

Katie's parents did begin to send us an occasional update and a few photos that we'd print out and put up on Amber's bedroom wall, so that her older sister could watch over her. But we didn't get into too many details with the parents, and kept our exchanges fairly casual. Once, after Amber had been with us for six months, I suggested that it would be a good idea to let the girls see each other at some point. Katie's mother replied to my email with a clear message: keep out of our family, you are not welcome. We talked to our social worker about the situation and she said that we should just keep in contact and hope that things get better in the future. So Katie has become an important, but absent, person in our lives, and we cannot help wishing that she lived with us, even though that was never a possibility.

When we were going through the adoption process, I thought a lot about both of Amber's parents. We knew their names, ages, backgrounds and even their likes and dislikes.

We felt, at first, like intruders into their lives, having to know so much about their sad and terrible childhoods and about their difficult relationship with one another. I had expected to hate any woman who could give away her babies so easily. But, of course, it wasn't like that. She didn't want to lose her children; in fact, part of the reason for having more was the hope that she might finally be allowed to keep one. Meanwhile, every inch of our growing towards being a family moved the birth parents further and further away. They were part of Amber's life, and so part of ours. But they were not, and never could be, central.

As time went on, and as we felt more confident in saying 'We are Amber's parents', we were able to thank the birth parents silently for giving us the precious gift of such a beautiful little girl. As promised in our agreement to maintain letterbox contact, we wrote to them towards the end of the first year, as we would every year, and sent a couple of photos. We tried to make the letter simple and interesting, without being patronising, but also knew that they might choose not to read it. It felt weird to write that letter: writing to strangers about whose lives we knew far too much. I tried to imagine that we were writing to a distant acquaintance and telling them about our children, not about theirs.

When we found out the couple had split up, we sent two copies of the letter. The social workers told us that the birth parents love their children and keep photos of them plastered all over their living room wall, like some sort of shrine. I did, and still do, lie awake sometimes at night wondering how we will cope with giving Amber more and more details about her birth parents. I am painfully aware that I can't protect her from this part of her story; and I'd be a liar if I said I don't want it all to go away sometimes, so that she won't have to hear hurtful answers to all those questions she'll have as she gets older. We decided, from the first couple of weeks she was with us, that regularly and frequently, without prompt, sometimes happily and sometimes reluctantly, we would make sure we told Amber about her tummy mummy and daddy. I show her photos of them, say how much they love her and wish they could have looked after her, but weren't able to.

I often tell Amber her story when she is splashing in the bath in the evenings, or playing with her dollies. I explain that she is special to have three mummies: tummy, foster and forever. And how lucky she is to have so many people who love her. The thing is, it's not easy to tell this story, but it *is* her story and she has a right to know the details. Drip by difficult drip, so that when she is old enough to understand, there'll be no great revelations, no unveiling of a terrible secret, no Auntie Hilda unwittingly giving away a serious piece of family gossip.

I remember a man on the preparation group saying that he didn't see why we had to be so open about adoption. We have photos dotted around the house of Amber's older sister, of her baby sister, and of her foster carers. For some reason I can't yet explain to myself, or to anyone else, we have a more private photo album of her birth parents and half-siblings. I'm not sure what anyone else would gain by seeing these photos right now, and feel that it should be Amber's right to choose to show them. Perhaps I'm afraid that people might start saying just how much Amber looks like her "real" dad, or has her "real" mum's eyes. But it may also be that I'm afraid of titillation: of casual observers making negative comments about the birth father's teeth or birth mother's hair. I want to protect them, in the sense that I want to protect Amber's right to love and respect them. I suppose I'm trying to say that I don't know what the birth parents will mean to Amber as she gets older, and until she knows that for herself, I don't want anyone else to make judgements about her birth parents on her behalf. I have made her a DVD of her life story and it's fun to watch. It charts her birth and even has a photo of the hospital she was born in, shows all her parents – birth to forever – and tells her about her first year with us, up until our first

Christmas. But although I like to show it to her as often as I can, it's kept in a secret place so that Grandpa and Grandma can't come across it and put it in the player inadvertently. I did once show my mum a photo of the birth parents and her reaction was exactly the same as mine. But the photo still went back into its dark box.

Dates have a different meaning for us these days. Whenever someone asks me Amber's date of birth, I struggle to remember it simply because it's not a key date in my life. We do have some very special dates that most other families don't share: the first day we saw her; the day introductions started; the day we brought her home; and the day of her adoption in court. Having an adopted child means that there are so many anniversaries to share besides birthdays and Christmas. For us, all these special events fall within a couple of months in the winter, so we have decided to inaugurate a family day in the middle of summer. On this day every year, we'll throw a huge party and invite all our friends to come and celebrate the fact that we are a family, and perhaps to make sure the entire planet knows just how much being a family means to us.

9

Are you a grandma yet?

My mum was in denial for many years.

'I'm far too young to be a grandma.' Or, 'I'm not ready to be a grandma, I've got too much to do.'

She watched, feeling a little helpless, as I struggled through years of infertility and frustration. She knew she couldn't say the right thing, but would have a go anyway. She soon gave up saying 'Just keep trying' or 'You need to relax a bit', as she would see the disapproval in my tired eyes. So she waited patiently, and just watched. And the more she kept her distance from me, the more she and my dad would just happen to find themselves in Mothercare, just happen to stare at every passing buggy, and just happen to linger in front of the display windows of every baby emporium. Until they'd start bumping into people they knew, who asked those innocent questions she loathed: 'Are you a grandma yet?'

She knew they'd be wondering what was wrong with me, and she'd revert to my tactic of muttering about international travel, being happy with my career and the usual bland dismissals she'd had plenty of time to perfect. So as the grandparents around her would rack up their numbers, my parents kept their empty count to themselves and tried really hard to convince themselves that it didn't matter, even though their daughter was hurtling through her thirties at breakneck speed.

One weekend when my parents came for a visit, I had a long chat with my mum over coffee in the garden. For the first time, she told me how hard it was for her. For a moment I was taken aback: wasn't this my problem? How could it possibly be as bad for her as it was for me? But that is not what she wanted or meant to say. She was trying to express her frustration at having to listen to the roll calls of her friends' grandchildren and to have to pass the baby shops with no reason to step inside. In fact, they'd made up a considerable mental shopping list before Amber arrived: our non-children already had a non-baby gym, a non-inflatable castle for the garden, next to the non-trampoline to jump on whilst wearing their trendy non-clothes. Not so deep down, of course, they were thoroughly miserable. Would they die without seeing grandchildren? Why had it happened to them? And then they started, very slowly and without really meaning it, to unload their frustrations onto us. Why *had* we left it so late? Hadn't we ever thought of trying earlier? What about when our friends were starting to have kids? Hadn't we been a bit irresponsible? So we told them the whole story and realised that all they wanted was to be able to help. And only when we'd talked everything through fully with them did we all feel better. Understanding our decisions, reluctances and frustrations put things into context for them. And it made David and me realise just how reluctant we were to ask for their help, but just how much we needed it.

When we first mentioned adoption, they were cautiously pleased for us. They knew that it could be a long and disappointing process, but also worried that it might turn out to be the wrong move for us. Were we really committed to the idea, or were we on the rebound from not being able to have our own child? They waited for our updates as we progressed towards approval, getting excited and deflated each time we did. Their unconditional support for us was great, and it meant a lot to be able to call my mum with any silly concern or hope. On the day we were approved, my mum whooped for joy and started to picture the little one who would soon be in their family too. At that moment I really understood what it meant to them.

'I was going to march into their office if they'd refused you,' she said, almost too excited to stand still at the phone on the other end. And after that, just like us, they would look at every toddler in the supermarket, thinking (out loud at times),

'We'd like that one,' or

'Not so keen on that (screaming) one.'

My mum and dad then lived about three hours away by car. But as soon as they retired they began planning their move to be nearer to us, to become hands-on grandparents. They were so pleased at the prospect of their soon-to-be new status that they barely registered the fact that they had both stopped doing jobs that had absorbed them for four decades. It took them over a year to sell and move, but finally the day came and they started a new life in a village about twenty minutes' drive from us. At that point we were having our house renovated, and before long they were hired as full-time decorators. When, in the midst of all this upheaval, we heard about Amber, my parents couldn't believe their luck. They returned to Mothercare, just to look at first, and then to come home from time to time with one or two 'bits for the baby'. Our excitement was fuelled by theirs, and our own frustrations were matched by theirs. We were definitely going through the process together.

The first time my parents saw Amber, she was playing with a doll on her bedroom floor during the introductions. They approached with smiling caution, so as not to upset her, but she was unperturbed by the presence of these curious strangers. She even let them hold her before they left ten minutes later. Soon my dad would sit on his settee at home impersonating his granddaughter, while my mum was boring her friends rigid with stories of her development. When Freya came along, they simply had double the material to draw on. I think if we'd asked them to move in with us, they'd have jumped at the chance.

David's parents were a bit different, and although they, too, loved Amber from the start, it was clear that they were not interested in taking a particularly hands-on approach to their second grandchild. Their life is neat, quiet, slow and ordered, so that our existence – with its animals, children and work – is just too much for them even to observe for any great length of time. They sit and drink tea, have lunch made for them, take their granddaughter out for a walk. And then they go home, leaving us to wash up their dishes and bathe the children. However, like my mum and dad, they loved Amber unconditionally from the start and with no sense that she was adopted and therefore different. They treated her in exactly the same way as their other granddaughter, Monica. I think they enjoyed the fact that our "baby" was already talkative and responsive, and they had a readymade little person to play with and entertain. The arrival of Freya was just as warmly welcomed by them, but they couldn't cope with both children at the same time. They prefer to take one of them out each week, and know that they would not be able to run around after two little toddlers without extra help from us. All in all, they want to enjoy their grandchildren, rather than take care of them.

Both grandmothers responded in the same way to Amber's first hospital episode. Within days of getting back to normal at home, they each started asking questions about how clean the house really was:

'Do you mop the floor often enough?'

'Is it good to have the cat food so close to the counter?'

'Do you clean the dog hairs up every day?'

They'd even been on the phone to one another to discuss our possible shortcomings. I was really annoyed and felt let down. Our close friends Neil and Jane had rushed to the hospital with homemade flapjacks and fresh espresso coffee, to tell us that we were doing fine, but our parents were too busy worrying about the state of our floors and grading our level of hygiene to be of any practical help. We see now that their concerns were out of love for this child, their granddaughter, and that they simply wanted her to get better. I did also tell them everything about the convulsion, so that the second emergency elicited much more support from them. We talk to them about the birth parents from time to time, but feel that it is their job to add roots to Amber's new family tree, while we ensure that the old one is protected and cherished.

My brother didn't want children: he is happy with his partner and dog. He is a gentle person, of few words, who always seems to be content in his own surroundings, with a small group of close and private friends. This is very different from me, always peopling my home with lovely faces and making sure that the world knows whether I'm happy or sad. So, if I had any expectations at all, it was that I didn't think he would be very good with the children. He came on his motorbike the first time to meet Amber, and when she saw the dark, be-leathered, bearded figure in the hall, she burst into tears and grabbed tightly at my jeans. Who wouldn't? After about twenty minutes, though, leathers off, drinking a cup of tea at the table and helping Amber open the presents he'd brought, he wasn't nearly so scary and before long she had him doing "Row a Boat". From then on, he would come when he could, even just for a quick visit, so that he could see his niece, and I got to know him a bit better than I had for quite a long time.

Uncle number two, David's brother Andrew, was already a father to Monica and was keen to show David how to be a good dad. He was happy and proud to help his older brother, and from the start was very good with Amber. Monica was just a couple of years older than

Amber, but had already been through the upheaval of divorce, so that she saw Andrew only every other weekend. Although a bit tough on Monica (and Andrew) at times, this arrangement is a contemporary reflection of the complicated lives children can lead. Monica just nodded when we told her that Amber had a little sister and a big sister, neither of whom lived with us. The world may seem to be getting more complex, but children are able to simplify it by removing all the emotional baggage and getting you down to raw facts. So Monica became a regular visitor too and Amber had a ready-made cousin to emulate. Monica pushed her to walk, and plays by sharing and by bossing her little cousin around from room to room.

Social workers give you a range of suggestions about introducing a newly placed child to friends and family. Some advise that you stay at home for one month. Others have very specific ideas about how many people should visit at any one time. We were guided by Amber, who was happy to be the centre of attention and was clearly used to having a variety of visitors. So Neil and Jane popped in and soon scooped her up with smiles. They were genuinely moved by our new parental status and have followed Amber's progress with love and interest ever since. They are part of Amber's family, as are John and Linda, whose own son was born only a couple of weeks before Amber arrived. They, too, seem to have a real love of children and don't stop for a moment to think about their origins, but value them as the weird and wonderful growing individuals they are. One or two friends dropped off, as you might expect in any change of circumstances. A couple we'd been out with fairly regularly just don't do children. They visited, brought presents and asked a few nice questions. But they were not really in their element, so we tried to meet them for dinner in various local pubs when we could get a babysitter. This, too, petered out after a few months. Another single friend was struggling with her own desire to have a baby and being around Amber didn't make her feel any better. I understood this feeling totally, so met her out for lunch a few times, but even this became too hard to sustain.

As old friends fizzled out of our lives, new ones appeared. The neighbour who'd helped out when Amber had her first fit turned out to be one of Amber's biggest fans. She and her two daughters, who would turn out to be fantastic babysitters, also became regular coffee-time visitors. Sometimes they would just pop in to say they hadn't seen Amber for a while, could they give her a hug? She, for her part, basked in such adulation and was gorgeous in their company. I can picture her going on holiday with them when she's older. And, most of all, Amber loves our friend Ellie, who indulges her with all the things we won't let her have often – chocolate, sweeties and crisps. Ellie comes over just for bath time, for play and cuddles, and Amber careers down the corridor to jump into her arms whenever she rings the bell. The two of them disappear off down the garden or into Amber's bedroom like teenage pals, in spite of the thirty-year age gap. Amber is as lucky to have so many special people around as she is to have her close family nearby. And although for now these people are her play buddies, in years to come many of them will be around to support her and encourage her with whatever life throws at her.

10

Here we go again

We were rolling along nicely as a family of three, but all the time we knew that a baby sister was growing and thriving. We knew because we kept in touch with Jim and Sue. Children's Services had made it clear that she was probably coming to live with us, and soon confirmed it as fact. We explained that if Freya could come in the summer, we would be able to spend a lot of time as a family of four. If she were delayed, then it would be much harder to organise, as David was preparing to take on a new contract, in part to make up for the time he was taking off now. I planned to take at least six months leave next time.

By the end of summer, Freya should already have been living with us. She was eight months' old and Amber was exactly one year older than her sister. I was angry at how we were being treated and felt yet again that adopters were at the bottom of the ladder of importance. We were dealing with exactly the same people as the first time around, but it was as though we'd never even met them before. So much had to be repeated. First we were told Freya would be placed in July, then August, then September, then October. It was getting ridiculous. Someone mislaid a medical report. There were court delays. We didn't dare book a long holiday, and were glad we'd gone ahead with the short Italian trip. We felt that nothing was moving forward and there seemed no prospect of starting life with Freya any time soon. So when Jim and Sue brought her to see us, we cooed and rocked her and pushed her round the garden on Amber's bike, while Amber herself showed off to the visitors. But all the time, I felt nothing for this baby. I am sure that this was a response to the uncertainty and lack of progress. A bit like moving house – we wouldn't quite believe that it would actually happen until we'd got the keys in our hands, or, in this case, had the baby handed to us. I was starting to regret that we'd slipped so easily into the process of number two. Perhaps we should have given ourselves more time to get used to the idea and to grow as a family with Amber. But it seemed natural that we should have her full sibling baby sister come and live with us.

One contact in Children's Services told us that we should be going ahead within weeks, but Freya's social worker then informed us that there would be no chance of that. In part to give myself something to do, I wrote a letter of complaint to Freya's local authority. Even the Independent Reviewing Officer frowned when we told him about the delays with Freya and said he saw no reason for them. I had also heard of couples being quickly approved as foster carers in cases such as ours. But, although we were surprised even to receive a response to my letter, it took us no further. As usual, no-one was responsible, nothing could be done, and all our fussing would get us nowhere. We moaned on, but nobody seemed to be listening. Anna was sympathetic, but she was too careful and diplomatic to want to rock the boat. We were without such diplomatic skills and made it clear to anyone who asked that we were not impressed. While we were going through the slow motions of making plans for Freya, Anna told us the latest news of the birth mother. She was pregnant again. We looked quizzically at her and she nodded:

'They'll more than likely come to you first, but you would need to think everything through and now is not the time to do that.'

Over the next few weeks we did start to think about it. Three children sounded great at one level, but terrifying at another. We were already sad that we couldn't have their older sister with us, but when would the babies stop? The mother was still quite young; do we take all of them? We more or less decided there and then that we would stop at two, at least for the foreseeable future. And somehow that gave us incredible relief, but at the same time made us determined to get on with Freya's placement using all the pressure we could bring to bear.

By September, things weren't looking good, and we started to hear murmurings of December. We had both had enough, and I lost my cool. How long could the waiting and uncertainty continue? We'd already missed the ideal time for us and David was now very busy with work. More importantly, how much was the authority paying to keep Freya in foster care for this unnecessarily long time? And, most importantly of all, was it in the interests of the child for her to wait even longer before joining her sister? Finally, I resorted to telling both Anna and Freya's social worker that we were thinking of pulling out, that they had pushed us just about as far as we could go, and that, for Amber's sake as much as ours, we needed to get on with the job of being an ordinary family. This wasn't an empty statement: I was making myself sick with anxiety and finding it hard just to get on with being a mum to Amber without worrying about her baby sister all the time. Miraculously, all persons concerned managed to convene a meeting with us the following week, and suddenly we had a date for matching panel and plans for introductions only four weeks later. Perhaps this was what they'd planned all along, or maybe they'd finally woken up to the fact that someone needed to take responsibility for securing Freya's future.

It was strange to return to Jim and Sue's house less than

ten months after the first set of introductions. We left Amber with my parents and set off without trepidation, with no concerns about whether Freya would take to us or whether the foster carers would be welcoming. We didn't even need to check the RouteMaster to see where we were going or how long it would take. And we stopped in our usual greasy spoon cafe when we arrived a little early. We played with Freya, now eleven months old, for a few hours on the first day, and even though she was understandably clingy to Sue, she soon warmed to our games and once or twice didn't even notice that Sue had left the room. Sue knew that we were planning to name her Emily, so had been using both names for a few months already.

The following day we took her to the same park we'd taken Amber to, played on the same swings Amber had enjoyed, and had a cup of tea in the same café we'd visited with her sister. She was three months younger than Amber had been during introductions, more baby-like and very cute. She fell asleep easily and cried only when we had to wake her to put her back in the car. On the third and fourth days we were already starting to get to know her personality. She was quieter, perhaps calmer, than Amber had been, but if anything more determined and more easily upset if she became frustrated. We soon realised that we had immediately started to compare the girls and that this wouldn't be very helpful, for them or for us.

We repeated the routine and Jim and Sue came over to stay in the same hotel. This time, though, they didn't have another baby to take care of and they felt strange to be on their own wandering around our town like lazy tourists. They began to get a sense of what it would be like to be without a baby in the house. By this time, the girls' birth mother had moved away to another area, so there was no likelihood of Sue being asked to care for the new baby. It didn't surprise us that they called a bit early to pick Emily up on the Sunday afternoon: they'd been twiddling their thumbs and just didn't know what to do with themselves.

Our experience of that weekend was the opposite of Jim and Sue's. They suddenly went from having one child to having no children around; we went from one to two in a moment. And both were moving around, busy and active. When they dropped Emily off on the Friday afternoon, Amber was still in the middle of her nap. We'd been in the playroom with the baby for twenty minutes when we heard Amber calling from her bedroom. Lifting her from her bed, David watched as Amber's expression changed from curiosity, to confusion and finally to disapproval. She'd heard her sister's voice and knew that someone was playing with her toys. She played reluctantly with Emily for an hour or so, was mildly put out at having to share her bath, and then seemed genuinely relieved to be left alone with us in the evening. We made sure we spoiled her, but there was no way we could prepare her for the changes to come.

For us, the shock was no less real. At one point during that afternoon, I stood in the hallway and looked at the two faces peering up at me. Amber was shouting at the top of her voice, demanding that I help her find some teddy or other, and Emily was crying while trying to poke her fingers into the electric socket. I suddenly wanted to swap with David; couldn't he take more time off work and leave me out of all this? It was too overwhelming; I didn't know where to start. How could I possibly give these two little girls everything they needed? I quickly took some Rescue Remedy – a natural stress reliever that social workers should hand out to all adopters – and took a deep breath. Then I went back to my children and tried to listen and to understand what each one needed.

The final day of introductions was very strange. We went for a walk in the village and down to the local children's farm. Along the way we met many people we hadn't seen for ages. One local woman, whom we only knew by her dog's name, looked confused.

'Two? I'd only ever seen the one,' she said. We didn't enlighten her, but hurried off instead to see the piglets and donkeys. Strange as it might have seemed to others, it was slowly beginning to seem normal to us and that dreadful feeling of impotence started to fade. It was just going to be more difficult with two, and we couldn't expect them to react in a similar way to what we did for them. The next day, when Jim and Sue left with Emily for the last time, we gave Amber all our attention for the rest of the afternoon and got her to help us to prepare her sister's room. Amber was a big sister now and we would need all the help she could give us.

And so on that Monday morning in October, we found ourselves back at the foster care centre, sitting at the same table with mostly familiar faces. Sue wasn't there, but had sent a report via Emily's social worker to say that introductions couldn't have been more perfect. Everyone else was satisfied that we were ready, and the meeting was closed almost as soon as it had begun. We signed a few papers and set off to Sue's village. This time we'd given her a precise time, so that she didn't have to hang around with a takeaway baby. We were early so looked for a place for lunch. We found what turned out to be some sort of British Legion club by night, but a regular café by day. It served good English fare and we were both ravenous. Neither of us was the least bit nervous, or even excited. Looking back, I don't think we could really believe that the day had finally come. We'd been numbed by months of procrastination and had been browbeaten into a kind of dull state. So we were relaxed as we waited for our order to arrive, although in the end the service was so slow that we had to leave our sandwiches and run back to the car. It was in those few minutes, driving to pick up our youngest daughter, that we were suddenly engulfed by the enormity of the moment. When we both walked into Sue's kitchen and saw our beautiful little baby, we finally melted and let ourselves believe that this was it. Emily came easily and happily into my arms, turning only once for a goodbye cuddle with Sue. Emily's social worker followed us out and hugged us before

I bundled the baby into the car and we drove away with our new precious cargo.

That was, of course, a day of agonies for Sue. She loved Emily, as she had loved Amber, just like a daughter. She'd had her almost from birth and now had to give her away. She knew that Emily was going to a good place, and that she would be with her sister, but the feeling of loss was very great. She and Jim had booked a holiday in the sun for the following week and tried to focus on that. They knew that we wanted them to play an important part in the lives of our children, and that we'd all have plenty of time in the months and years ahead to catch up.

Visits by the social workers only just met the minimum statutory requirement this time round: nobody was worried about us; they knew that the girls were thriving and they had serious cases that needed their utmost attention. So they came, had coffee and cake, admired the girls and left. Emily's local authority had agreed to pay our travel expenses during introductions, as they had done with Amber. But this time they tried to give us a smaller amount than we'd been given previously, as if prices had gone down and not up. They were quibbling over a few pounds with us, but had been happy to pay for months and months of additional foster care, and seemed not to realise that we would take Emily on for the rest of our lives with one hundred per cent responsibility for her physical, mental and financial well being. Once again, we were being made to feel that we should be grateful to be getting the family we had so desperately wanted. And we do feel very lucky that things have turned out so well, but a little bit of appreciation of adopters as a valuable part of adoption would have helped at times.

Our triumph as a family unit coincided with a much-postponed appointment with the consultant gynaecologist. We'd almost forgotten about the treatment and tests in all the stress of the adoption process. That process itself had taken its toll on my health. During the two adoptions, I lost about a stone in weight, caught unshakeable 'flu and came almost to the point of throwing crockery once or twice with the sheer frustration of it all. So when the new appointment came through, I was perfectly happy to close the treatment chapter. The consultant ran through the tests we'd both had and concluded that our best and final chance to have a child would be to have another go at IVF as soon as possible. He barely registered the fact that we had in the meantime adopted one child and were three days away from adopting another one. He stressed that time wasn't on my side and insinuated that I had already wasted valuable months and years by messing about with the adoption route. He was cold and unfeeling and completely stunned me, and I had to hold David's hand to stop myself from crying. I didn't want any more attempts at treatment, but he made it all sound so final that as I walked out of the consulting room I wanted to collapse on the nearest red plastic chair. We sat quietly for a few minutes, before I took a deep breath and just said:

'No more of this. Let's go and pick up our daughter.' And a hug from her really was the best tonic. I knew that I'd visited the gynaecology clinic for the last time.

11

And then there were two

On 25 December 2006, we were a couple with a promise of an adopted child. Exactly one year later, our parents came – as grandparents – to spend Christmas Day with their children and their children's children. We were suddenly – very suddenly – a family of four and life was so hectic we hardly had the chance to appreciate our new status. We are in an unusual situation: Amber and Emily not only came to us in quick succession, but came like a pair of candlesticks, a matching set. We joke that we have our supermarket children – buy one, get one free. And we didn't have too much time to wonder whether or not it was really a good idea. Emily had been asleep on the dining room table in Sue's house the first time we visited Amber at home. And, at least subconsciously, she had become part of our family when her older sister did. This makes it easy for us to prepare and deliver life story work. We can talk to them together, often when they're in the bath, telling them the story of three little sisters. They will always have the same blood, the same history, and the same concoction of tummy and forever mummies and daddies.

On a different level, I ask myself if this makes them exclusive. They have, in some ways, something that David and I will never share with them: they have each other as full blood relatives. But it is too simplistic to think that way: they have a full blood older sister whom they never see, while Amber mimics me, sounds like me and increasingly looks like me. Interestingly, the absence of the older sister, Katie, makes Amber the older child, a role she fills fully and with verve. I am not sure she would have made such a good middle child. Moreover, Emily is the image of Katie, while she and Amber look only vaguely alike. So they are related, but I'm not sure how significant that is. What makes me happy is that my girls share the same life story and do not have to face it alone. So whenever they reflect on being adopted, or feel the need to search out their birth parents (although we'd be happy to help them there), they can share any fear or anxieties with one another. They are a protective mechanism for each other, should they need one. They come from exactly the same mould. In that sense, they are very lucky sisters.

Amber did not feel at all lucky when Emily first came to join us. She was very jealous, followed me around all the time and wouldn't leave me alone. Strangely, she rejected David, who'd spent all those months attending to her every need. It may have been because he was suddenly busy with work and so didn't spend all day long with her. But it was more likely due to the fact that I was paying so much attention to this infant ball of noisiness. Amber would cling to my trouser legs; she'd throw herself into my arms saying 'Baby'; and wanted me to feed her as if from a bottle. She demanded constant cuddles and reassurances. So we indulged her until she got used to the idea that Emily was here to stay. She was soon saying 'Sis' and before long wanted to rush to her sister's bedroom to wish her good morning.

For David and me, the only occasionally looming regret was that Katie wasn't also part of our family unit. Of course, we hadn't known about Katie's existence until we heard about Amber, and she was placed before we were even approved as adopters, so there was never any chance that she could have come to us. But we couldn't, and can't, help feeling sad that this lovely sister isn't with her two siblings and can't enjoy the togetherness they share. When I was little and complained about my baby brother, my mum used to say, 'He's the only brother you've got'. When Amber pushed her baby sister one day, I said, 'She's the only sister you've got,' but had to add quickly, 'living with you'. For them, there will have to be degrees of sisterhood: Amber lives with Emily and is bound to be closer to her, while Katie – hopefully, given time – will become like a cousin we see occasionally. We put a photograph of Katie in each of our girl's rooms, so that they know she is a special person for them.

We realised that comparing the girls' development would be inevitable. Amber did not walk until she was twenty months old, but Emily was running about by fourteen months. Emily had Amber as a role model, and maybe she was just determined to keep up with her sister. At the ages of one and two, they are already very different from one another and we keep reminding ourselves that children are individuals and will just do things when they are ready.

Amber still struggles to understand that she can't have Mummy to herself all the time and that, although she insists that I'm exclusively hers, she has to share me with Emily. At times they play together like little angels, making noises and banging the nearest table or box. And at other times, especially when she thinks we're not looking, Amber will nudge her sister out of the way, or even try to push her over. These are neither more nor less than the normal reactions of an older sibling who has to get accustomed to the arrival of a new baby. But we made it clear that Emily was with us for good.

Adjustment to Emily's arrival was difficult for all of us. At first, I was excited at the prospect of being away from work, of being able to enjoy home life with my children and of getting to know Emily on the days when Amber went to nursery. But I soon started to feel that it was hard to bond with Emily and began to resent her for not being more like her sister. I'd got used to Amber's demanding behaviour, but Emily's whining was intolerable at times. Instead of the dream of family life I'd harboured, my life seemed to be punctuated by screaming, whingeing and tears. I was beginning to think that I didn't love Emily, and wondered whether I could ever feel about her as I did about Amber. The whole situation was exacerbated by the reactions of friends and family, who all kept telling me what a cute and perfect baby Emily was, how calm and quiet and how smiley. But none of them was around at 5pm, when Amber could be found tearing up and down the wooden floor of the long hall, while Emily was sitting in the middle and just crying or moaning. I could never cook food quickly enough to satisfy them, and would often try to fill their tummies, get them in the bath and put them to bed as soon as possible. I couldn't wait for that end-of-day peace and tranquillity.

Those difficult weeks became even harder when Amber contracted chickenpox. My mind had invented so many lovely stories about life with my adopted children, but one scenario I hadn't envisaged was that I would get chickenpox in my late thirties, thanks to my young daughters. I glanced at myself in the mirror one evening, ten days after Amber had contracted the disease and only two days after she'd returned to nursery. I couldn't believe my eyes when I saw three pinkish spots on my chest. I took off my shirt to see that I was completely covered, and at that moment my scalp began to itch, too. I was quite poorly with it, and felt very low and lethargic. It took me a couple of weeks to begin to feel better, but by then I was starting to worry about how we would cope when I returned to work at the end of my adoption leave. As I was getting better, Emily also caught chickenpox. Meanwhile David was getting home late most evenings, and was also getting 'flu.

One Sunday morning, after no sleep whatsoever for the grown-ups, and snatches of rest for the not-quite-right toddlers, we just made up the sofa bed at 9am and all four of us fell asleep for an hour. When I look back at that moment, trying not to think about the facial scars I may never lose, it was a real family time. Families get sick. Together. And they all have to cuddle up and get better.

We both came to realise that we depended more or less on our full energy levels just to keep up our normal routine, and that any obstacles – such as illness – required spare capacity we scarcely possessed. The good thing about all of this was the realisation that I wasn't resentful of Emily, I was just finding it almost impossible to cope with two such young children. Feeling better, I looked at Emily with fresh eyes and we soon regained a happier equilibrium.

Throughout this time, we continued with our voluntary work and visited Jason whenever we could. Amber soon came to adore him and would squeal with joy when we told her we were going to play with him. With the dog, two toddlers, car seats and a buggy, Saturday mornings with Jason were not easy. But he was so happy to see the girls, ran round and round the park with them and would often bring them small gifts, so that there was no way we could stop seeing him. He has already told Amber that he's sort of adopted too, and that he will be a special friend – 'like a cousin' for her and her sister. Jason will be a close family friend for as long as he wants to spend time with us, and we hope that will mean forever.

In preparation for my return to work, we enrolled Emily in Amber's nursery for three days a week, like her sister. They were in separate classes but the teachers would often bring them together, for singing or during outdoor playtime. From the start, both girls loved the nursery and it wasn't long before Amber was asking to go to "school" even on days when they were at home. During this trial period, I was not at work but instead was preparing in advance some of the teaching I would have to do. One lunchtime, during Emily's second week at nursery, the phone rang. It was Lisa, the teacher from Emily's class, calling to let me know that Emily had a very high temperature and was lying quite motionless on the floor. Both my parents and David's were on holiday and David had had to go down to London for a meeting, where he had evidently switched off his phone. I felt so alone. Emily was no better when I got to the nursery, but even in her limp state she managed to smile at me as I walked in. I held her and felt a huge surge of relief that she was safely in my arms.

I called the doctor when I got home and described Emily's symptoms. He was fairly convinced that she just had a cold, but told me to monitor her and bring her to the surgery if I wanted to. I was trying not to think of Amber's convulsions. I felt such huge responsibility and in the end phoned the neighbour to see if she'd come and play with Amber for a few minutes, so that I could just hold her baby sister. I remembered that in our preparation group we'd done an exercise where I'd been given an inflated balloon to hold. And then another. And another. And another. Soon my arms were full, but it hadn't occurred to me to ask anyone to give me a hand. The point of the exercise was to learn how to ask for help when you need it, and I was glad that I felt able to do that now.

Later that evening, when Emily seemed to be back to normal, I took my reaction as a sign of the strengthening bond between us. I realised that I do love Emily, and that our relationship with Amber is just more mature, more developed and, for now, a bit deeper.

Whether or not you have them from birth, looking after two children so close in age is demanding and challenging most of the time. We are sure that we face many of the same problems any parent would have to deal with in having two close siblings. At one and two years old, they cannot appreciate why we tell them to take care. And so we have literally been pulling Amber away from a near-encounter with unfriendly cat claws while Emily is about to trap her fingers in the door. They can't be left alone for more than one-and-a-half minutes (our record) at the moment. As they are both unable to express themselves fully, they often get frustrated if they can't make themselves understood. Throw in the "terrible twos", and we have a lot of tantrums and tears, particularly when they're tired. Being so close in age also means paying a fortune for nursery care for two children at once. But our hope is that this small age gap will turn out to be a major advantage to both of them as they grow older. We like to imagine that they'll be good friends through their teenage and college years, and way beyond. It will be up to them to make this happen, but they are already showing positive signs of becoming great sisters.

In regard to their adoptive status, the age range will make it easier for us to liaise with schools in the future; with luck, we'll only have to explain our situation once to the heads and their staff. For us, having them so close together made sense. We could deal with the same authorities, with the same individuals within those authorities, and adopting the second time round was very easy in terms of understanding procedures and arranging the practicalities of the placement. And, although it can be hard at times to cope with the high-pitched, constant demands of pre-verbal toddlers, we have everything we need and feel mentally prepared for Emily's development as she trots behind Amber's short lead. Ours has been a happy and relatively straightforward path to adoption, precisely because we have been matched with young toddlers who've had a great start in life.

We have had no transition problems, and any issues that do arise relate to the fact of suddenly becoming parents, not to the fact of becoming parents to adopted children. We can't relate to the sad stories of adoption breakdown, of attachment traumas, or to those parents who have to face difficult issues of adjustment even years after placement.

There are many wonderful people able to adopt children with challenging behavioural and physical needs, and we always knew that we would not be ready or able to cope with such problems. We knew our limitations and we also knew that we could look after young children and give them everything they needed. We can live with a shadow family always in the background of our daughters' lives; after all, we don't own or possess children, we just borrow them, whether they come from inside us or from adoption agencies. But having had such a problem-free transition to family life does mean that we rarely think of ourselves as anything but a regular, easy-going and solid family unit.

Being one of two girls so close in age, almost like twins, can have its disadvantages, but, so far at least, they are very different. Amber is a boy in a girl's body: she is boisterous and energetic, and crashes into her world to discover it. Emily, in contrast, sits quietly and observes, computing every detail of the scenes around her. She risks being the forgotten child at times, as Amber can be all-consuming and monopolises every ounce of attention. But then Emily will do something small but remarkable, like the first time she decided to take a few steps. She is no second best, and will make sure we always know it.

While I was off work being a full-time mum, I really enjoyed being able to watch the children grow and, like David, I would structure my days around a cluster of self-contained activities: Monday to toddlers group, Tuesday swimming, and so on. I gradually began to make friends at the local playgroup, got over my phobia of other women's birth stories and realised that most of them face exactly the same challenges as I do from day to day. They offered useful tips when I was worried that Emily was eating too much, or that Amber's behaviour was about to get her expelled from nursery. She'd got into a habit of pushing other children, so that whenever I heard crying I'd look up and assume Amber to be the culprit. She was, my new friends assured me, turning into a normal two-year-old. So while Amber barged her way through daily life, her no-longer baby sister was starting to grow into a quietly confident little girl. She wasn't that interested in playing with the other children at the toddlers group, but preferred to take a selection of toys into a corner, where she'd occupy herself for quite a while.

The playgroup, although not outwardly aiming at religious education, was based around the church and I began to talk to the organisers about teaching the Bible to young children. We do not go to church and are never quite sure what to put on forms; "Christian" usually does the general trick, but we don't really think about religion. At the same time, though, we both feel that the teachings of the Christian church form an important part of our civilisation and history and we do want the girls to know the story of Jesus. We would also consider having them christened in the next couple of years, and want to give them the chance to grow up as Christians. It will be up to them to stay in or opt out when they get older. So for now, we have a colourful children's Bible and say a little prayer of thanks for each day we have together. Amber gives a resounding and enthusiastic 'Aaaaaaaaaa-men' before bedtime.

During my time at home, we also got into food in a big way. Most days would see us all cooking and baking, usually with pink or black icing as a finishing touch. Amber loved to stir the mixture and both of them (and David if he was at home) couldn't wait to lick the bowl. They understood that the cooker was very hot and not to be touched, and Amber would go and fetch the oven gloves for me to put her cakes in. Those moments reminded me of my own childhood, learning to make cakes with my mum and grandma. And they were exactly the kind of moments I'd dreamed of for so long. On some days David would come into the kitchen to be welcomed by a counter full of pies, fairy cakes and ginger biscuits. The house smelled delicious. Both girls also loved to eat vegetables and we would chop, slice, liquidise, fry, grill and roast a whole range of colourful veggies from our organic box each week. Amber often came back from nursery and asked for 'Soooooooup'. As we are bringing them up as vegetarians, it is important for them to understand about food and where it comes from. Their little pots are ready for spring, when they will grow their own tomatoes, beans and watercress. We know that they will come across meat – and highly processed meat at that – at birthday parties and elsewhere, and we're not worried about them eating a few hot dogs. They will make up their own minds about their lifestyle eventually; all we can do is to explain to them why we have chosen to live as we do. For now, though, they are thriving and glowing on the wholesome diet at home and at the nursery, and that's all we can hope for.

As I prepared to return to work, we both began to dread the logistical nightmare of managing children, commuting and having careers. We decided to inject some military precision into our daily routines, and each evening we'd get everything ready for the following morning. At the same time, though, I was excited about getting my teeth back into an adult world and having a side to my life that does not involve having a small child attached to one of my legs at all times. It did take us a few weeks to get used to the new regime and some mornings were simply chaotic, as the girls piled, late, into the car with non-matching socks and unwiped faces. But, like every other family, we soon got used to our new life and we all look forward to doing our own thing during the week and to our special time together at the weekend.

Such organisation depends heavily on an intricate arrangement for childcare. They go to nursery together three days a week, and we decide at the start of each week which of us will do the drop-off and pick-up, depending on our own schedules. The other two days involve grandparents and are therefore more flexible and more difficult. I work at home on Mondays and my parents come over, which means that they can stay with the girls, but know that I am only in the study if they need me. Fridays see the parallel arrangement for David and his parents. The reality of this potentially ideal solution is that sometimes our parents are on holiday, sick, or otherwise engaged and we are already looking into the possibility of sending the girls to nursery five days a week. Even when they are at nursery, someone has to be at hand in case they need to be picked up. As my parents live near to us, they have always been willing to do an emergency run. Otherwise, David is often at home and therefore closest to the nursery. But we have to review our plan for each week, as it may change slightly, in order to make sure that Amber and Emily are never too far from one member of their family or another.

12

Reflections

I cannot say that the adoption process has all been plain sailing; that we would go through it readily again in order to have another child; or that we'd never raised our voices – or blood pressure – in dealing with the authorities. We do understand how couples fall along the wayside, as there is so much room for disappointment and distress.

We were overwhelmed at times by the incompetence of the people holding the keys to our future. Harassed, over-worked and sometimes insensitive individuals have such power over your lives that it can be hard to find a way of clawing back control, because you feel that you are ruled by a faceless, bureaucratic structure. There is so much waiting, there are so many delays, nobody keeps you informed and when they do they may tell you different things. These people go home at night and watch TV, or deal with their own family problems; they do not have to live with adoption twenty-four hours a day. The only thing to do is to keep busy with work, with holidays, with house redecorating, doing all the things you won't be able to do as easily once that child arrives.

For most would-be adopters, and especially those who want to be matched with very young children, approval is the beginning of a period of silent waiting. There is no communication or, worse, there are false hopes of children whose needs you cannot meet. And you can soon get to the point where you don't think it will ever happen. Looking back, of course, we had to wait only eight months. But at the time we were constantly fighting off nagging fears that we would never become parents.

The process of matching once a child has been identified can be confusing and upsetting, too. And if you have to deal with two agencies – one for you and one for your child – then the problems can be doubled. Before Amber came home to us, we had to persuade various social workers and ourselves that we could and would love and take care of this little girl. We thought about every aspect of our lives and how she would fit into it. And we saw so many photographs and heard so much about her that she drew us into her life somehow. Yet we were powerless and had no say in decisions about her future with us. What should have been happy and exciting weeks of anticipation were, for us, very trying and painfully long. With hindsight, it may seem that we were expecting things to move too quickly, but when you're living through every day of waiting it is very hard to sit back and let others plan your life for you. Over and above all the hassle and frustration, you occasionally remember that you are about to embark on the most life-changing event: about to take one hundred per cent responsibility for a little person. Forever. Waves of self-doubt and hesitancy can sweep you off course just as easily as the mini-battles with Children's Services.

If we had to go through this process again we would be less forthcoming. We were too open and quick to give information beyond the direct questions we were asked. Sometimes we felt as though we were being judged about some of the more fundamental life choices we had made, and rather than engaging in a discussion about why we felt that way, or what the implications would be for a child, we were met with a wall of disapproval. We learnt the hard way that had we not explicitly mentioned that we were vegetarians, an assumption that we eat meat would probably have been made and we could have carried on with our plans once Amber arrived without all the fuss in the interim. If there is no prescribed policy on a given issue, discussions can turn into very personal disagreements about different approaches to child rearing. Of course, as emotionally hyperactive prospective adopters, we probably over-analysed the process and our approach to it. In some ways this is an inevitable consequence of a requirement to reflect on so many aspects of your life. But it is very important not to eat, sleep and breathe adoption every day of the week, and to ensure that you stay on track and think through the practicalities involved, rather than constantly turning it into a set of emotional issues.

More fundamentally for us, the biggest mistake we made was to go down the IVF route first. If I had my chance again I would say no to that option. It works for many people and is an amazing opportunity, but we wish we had thought more seriously about adoption at the start, instead of first dismissing it and then seeing it as a last resort. Of course, adoption is not for everyone. IVF isn't for everyone. Children aren't for everyone. We have to decide who we are and where we want to go, and how to get there. Only when Amber arrived did I really think I'd found what I'd always been looking for, and when I said as much to David he just nodded in agreement. It had taken us a long time to reach that point.

However slowly we felt we progressed (and regressed) on our way towards adoption, within twenty-six months of going to the first preparation group we had already become a family of four. Most birth parents would struggle to match that timetable. And when we look at Amber and Emily every night as they lie sleeping, we still have to pinch ourselves to believe our good fortune. They are our precious daughters and we have not had one moment of doubt about our decisions. More than that, the thought of life without either of them is, truly, unbearable.

Taking a calmer view now of what we have had to go through to reach this point, we can see how the authorities overreacted at times, how we overreacted at other times, and how everyone involved can become frustrated by timetables and systems set up by invisible others. We do appreciate now that if the system let us – and the children – down from time to time, we did meet several great individuals who went over and above their job descriptions to help us. Most of all, we learned a lot about Anna, our social worker, and our first impression of her – perhaps like her first impression of us – was enhanced significantly during the months we spent together. And if we are not best friends at the end of this process, we have a good, friendly relationship based on a deep mutual respect. Dana, Amber's social worker, too, turned out to be a very special person who genuinely cared that we should become a new family. Perhaps because she was about to become a grandmother herself, or maybe because she is just kind and generous, she went out of her way to call us late at night, or send updates and photos by email. With hindsight, I think that the best way to get through the process is to target and cling to key individuals and to realise that they, too, are struggling with a system that often malfunctions. At the end of it all, the day of the final court hearing comes with a huge sense of relief and freedom: no more singing to someone else's tune. The court date for Emily's adoption is scheduled for this week, and that day will mark the very first moment when we can really be the independent family we have always wanted to be.

The most important people in successful adoption, its secret weapon, are the foster carers. The start they give to children can set them on a secure and happy path to a healthy life. They are mother and father to your child while you are waiting. They have to deal with Children's Services on a daily basis and live with the knowledge that the little ones in their care will move on. Sue and Jim are very experienced foster carers and we were very lucky that they took care of our girls. Amber and Emily were full members of their family and had the best possible start in life thanks to these special people. Objectively, even if it went against our interests sometimes, we understand why social workers wanted to take their views so seriously to keep them happy. There are many waiting adopters, but good foster carers are like gold to be treasured. Some foster carers do not have too much contact, if any, with the children once they've moved on to their adoptive home. And we could also have chosen to cut the ties. But we all decided that it would be in the best interests of the children to have regular – if infrequent – contact with Jim and Sue. We hope that they will always want to join us for our family party, and to meet up with us once or twice a year just to keep in touch. We know that we owe their birth mother and father for the very existence of our daughters, but we also owe Jim and Sue for giving them such a wonderful first year of life.

I'd like to think this is a success story for all of us. Amber and Emily share a story. They live a warm life together, are happy, healthy and much loved. In many ways, we took the easiest route by adopting infants. An infant has little memory of what has gone before and is more likely to adjust quickly and easily to a new family environment. Under-twos may keep you up longer at night, may require you to change nappies and are not able to express themselves verbally. But there are less likely to be adjustment and attachment problems and we felt that we quickly settled into being just like any other family. At the same time, we have had to make some serious adjustments to what we now realise was a leisurely lifestyle before children. We can't go into work at a time that suits us if it doesn't suit the nursery. We can't say yes to plans without consulting with multiple home and work diaries. We can't even go to the pictures spontaneously, as babysitters generally need to have more than five minutes' notice.

David was born to be a father, and he is thriving in the

role. He has slipped very easily and naturally into his daddy skin and feels complete, thanks to our girls. Every night if he can, he'll still come with me into their rooms, where we'll just hold hands and look at the sleeping beauties in front of us. He feels a huge sense of responsibility for them, but also an enormous sense of pride that we are raising two lovely little people. And I am now a real mummy, who changes nappies and does more washing than the army each week, and who has to pinch herself as she walks down the street with her husband and daughters.

Meanwhile, the girls' birth mother has had another child, another little girl. We were positive that we would simply say no to any more children. Our hands are pretty full as it is and we have had to go through so much to get this far, to become a complete and happy family. But the child is no longer an imagining, she's a sister to our little girls and could fit right into the home we've made. There are so many arguments against putting ourselves forward: other adopters may be waiting, just as we were, for a baby to come along; we want to give our children all the attention they need; a third child may feel isolated from the two bonded sisters; and, after all, we may not be deemed to be suitable. Wouldn't we be mad to have three girls under three? And yet something deep inside prevented me from saying 'No, thank you' when I received that phone call. This little girl is, one way or another, part of our family. Amber and Emily have settled in so easily and so completely that we have now reached a point where we could contemplate going through it all again. I thought that David would bring me to my senses and veto the possibility, but he, too, feels quite ambivalent. The confused feelings we have right now are probably the same for any adopters who are offered a sibling to their adopted child or children. How can we deny the possibility for brothers and sisters to be together, to grow up as the family they would have been in other circumstances? But we have to weigh everything up very seriously and not be driven by an emotionally charged desire to make things better. If we have to say 'no', I know I'll feel a huge loss. We're far from making a decision, but it has shocked both of us that we feel so strongly about a little person we've never seen and know very little about. Having to decide whether to keep sisters together or separate them forever is proving more difficult than anything we have done so far.

Has it all lived up to the dream? Well, the dream didn't bother to mention the tantrums, the tears, the exhaustion or any illness. But nor did it prepare us for the depth of feeling we would have for our little precious girls. It's noisier, and definitely smellier, than I'd imagined. At times it is also quite banal; in dreams we don't have to eat, sleep and go to the toilet so often. But the reality is also funnier, and more amazing, and nothing is taken for granted in our daily routine. We just look forward to every day of having them with us for as long as they want to hang around.

As I sit at the kitchen table finishing this book, David and the girls are playing noisily on the floor beside me. Amber is counting pencils: 'One, two, three, eight, ten', while her sister is emptying the shoe box by the back door and spraying mud all over the place. When she looks up at Amber, Emily is offered a blue pencil and responds with a raspberry, setting both of them off into raptures of giggles. They are so firmly and clearly sisters, permanent playmates and soul mates for the future. The kitchen is in chaos and the sound of raspberry blowing fills the air. Putting the final full stop to this book, I can't think of anywhere I'd rather be right now.